SHROPSHIRE
& STAFFORDSHIRE

Extracted from

AN INVENTORY OF NONCONFORMIST
CHAPELS AND MEETING-HOUSES
IN
CENTRAL ENGLAND

PREFACE

Nonconformist places of worship have for some years been the subject of detailed investigation by the Royal Commission on the Historical Monuments of England, and the records accumulated, nation-wide, will be available in the archives of the National Monuments Record. The following pages form part of the first published volume resulting from these investigations, *An Inventory of Nonconformist Chapels and Meeting-houses in Central England* (HMSO 1986). This is, however, a substantial volume, and for reasons of convenience and local interest it has also been divided into county fascicules for individual publication and separate sale, the pagination of the full *Inventory* being retained.

The subject is taken to include not only the Old Dissent of Presbyterians, Independents, Baptists and Quakers but also the New Dissent of the 18th century, the Methodists and Moravians, together with denominations of more recent origin.

Over the years denominational names have been subject to alteration: some by re-grouping, notably with the formation in 1972 of the United Reformed Church (URC); others by the more gradual process of reunion and doctrinal evolution. Original doctrinal names have, where possible, been used throughout, subsequent changes being noted in the text except in the case of Methodist groups of which only a few remained independent after 1932.

The work of investigation and recording of nonconformist places of worship, for archive and publication, has been entirely the responsibility of Mr Christopher Stell of the Commission staff. Much of it was completed before the changes in local government boundaries of 1974, and in *Inventory* and fascicules the county names and boundaries obtaining immediately prior to that date have been retained.

ABBREVIATIONS

NMR   National Monuments Record
RCHM   Royal Commission on the Historical Monuments of England
URC   United Reformed Church

BIBLIOGRAPHICAL SOURCES
other than those fully titled in the text

SHROPSHIRE AND STAFFORDSHIRE

Barker, J. *c*.1910	*Shrewsbury Free Churches* [*c*. 1910].
Black, K. M. 1906	*The Scots Churches in England.*
Chambers, R. F. 1963	*The Chapels of the Industrial Midlands*: vol. IV of *The Strict Baptist Chapels of England* (5 vols, 1952–68).
CHST	*Transactions of the Congregational Historical Society*, 21 vols (1901–72).
CYB	*The Congregational Year Book* (Congregational Union of England & Wales), from 1846.
Drysdale, A. H. 1889	*History of the Presbyterians in England.*
Elliot, E., ed. 1898	*A History of Congregationalism in Shropshire.*
Evans, G. E. 1897	*Vestiges of Protestant Dissent.*
Evans, G. E. 1899	*Midland Churches: A History of the Congregations on the Roll of the Midland Christian Union.*
Kendall, H. B. 1905	*The Origin and History of the Primitive Methodist Church*, 2 vols [1905].
Matthews, A. G. 1924	*The Congregational Churches of Staffordshire.*
Reavley, J. 1925	*Presbyterianism in Shrewsbury and District, 1647–1925.*
Seymour, A. C. H. 1839	*The Life and Times of Selina, Countess of Huntingdon* [Seymour, A. C. H.], 2 vols.
Sibree, J. & Caston, M. 1855	*Independency in Warwick.*
Stuart, D. G. 1971	'The Burial-grounds of the Society of Friends in Staffordshire', *Trans. South Staffs. Archaeol. & Hist. Soc.*, XII (1970–1) 37–48.
Sturge, C. D. *et al.* 1985	*An Account of the Charitable Trusts ... Belonging to Friends of Warwick, Leicester and Stafford Quarterly Meeting.*
UHST	*Transactions of the Unitarian Historical Society* (from 1917).
VCH	Victoria History of the Counties of England, *Shropshire*, 4 vols (1908–79), in prog.
Wood, J. H. 1847	*A Condensed History of the General Baptists of the New Connexion.*

ISBN 0 11 300011 1

Printed for HMSO by Acolortone Ltd C35 6/86 Dd.736262

With the exception of the Baptist cause in Bridgnorth, and that of the Baptists and in some degree the Independents in Shrewsbury, the oldest surviving nonconformist congregations in the county are all of Presbyterian origin. Their varied fortunes are most clearly exemplified in the history of the High Street congregation in Shrewsbury (88), which was repeated at Wem (108) and at Whitchurch (113), all of which suffered the loss of a meeting-house in the riots of 1715 and were the scene of doctrinal divisions and secessions later in the same century; at Bridgnorth (6), however, in the southern half of the county, divisive influences are less apparent. The origins of the Independent congregation in Ludlow (49) about 1736 and of the Baptist church at Broseley (8) in 1741 are of interest as indicating the continued vitality of the older dissent immediately prior to the spread of Methodism. With this last the name of John Fletcher of Madeley will always be associated; although he remained vicar of Madeley from 1760 until his death in 1785, Fletcher's peripatetic and enthusiastic ministry (27, 28) laid the foundations of many of the Methodist societies in the industrial region east of Shrewsbury in which the parish of Dawley predominates. In the same area the Quaker meetings near Ironbridge (9, 18) received much support from the Darby family, ironmasters of Coalbrookdale.

The oldest surviving chapels in Shropshire are fragmentary or much altered and even those of the late 18th century are more remarkable for their age than their architecture; of these the former Congregational chapel in Market Drayton (51), of 1778, is externally the most complete. Some architectural pretention is found in the chapels of the early 19th century such as Newport (60), of 1832, and Ebenezer Chapel, Shrewsbury (95), built by the Methodist New Connexion in 1834, both in the Classical manner, and in the later part of the century in the Gothic designs of Bidlake of Wolverhampton (52, 89, 91) and Spaull of Oswestry (68, 70), while R. C. Bennett's Romanesque chapel in Shrewsbury (96), of 1870 is a natural sequel to his Congregational chapel in Gloucester Street, Weymouth, Dorset, of ten years earlier. Also notable, as an instance of private patronage, is the chapel built by Thomas Barnes at The Quinta (110). Many of the country chapels of the 19th century are small three-bay buildings of which Welshampton (105), of 1832, is an example of a type which continues into the later part of the century, e.g. (39), (55), (107), with some slight increase in the degree of elaboration.

Walling materials in the eastern parts of the county are generally brick but rubble occurs in the south and west while some use of impressively large blocks of sandstone is found in the north, e.g. (59), (75). Polychrome brickwork of the later 19th century is especially noticeable in the vicinity of Dawley; yellow, white, blue, red and brown brick being used in various contrasting combinations. Cast-iron window frames are particularly frequent in the county, including geometrically-patterned glazing bars in the later years, e.g. (30), (55), (107), and the same material is used at Broseley (6) for funerary monuments.

BASCHURCH

(1) PRIMITIVE METHODIST, Walford Heath (SJ 446200). Built 1841, extended at front and date-tablet reset.

BAYSTON HILL

(2) Former CONGREGATIONAL, Baystonhill (SJ 486088). Rendered walls and slate roof; three-bay front, gabled centre bay with tablet inscribed 'MOUNT PLEASANT 1834' above former arched entrance. Doorway re-sited at end in late 19th century. (URC)

Elliot (1898) 247–8.

(3) Former CONGREGATIONAL, Lyth Hill (SJ 467067). Brick and slate, now rendered and converted to a house, formerly entered at the S end, no original features survive. Reputedly built c.1800, but possibly later.

Elliot (1898) 175–6.

BERRINGTON

(4) PRIMITIVE METHODIST, Cross Houses (SJ 539075). Built 1836, transferred to Methodist New Connexion 1839 and renamed 'Ebenezer'.

VCH *Shropshire* VIII (1968) 27.

BRIDGNORTH

(5) BAPTIST, West Castle Street (SO 716930). The chapel, rebuilt in 1842 by a congregation in existence since c.1700, has brick walls and a rendered front of three bays separated by paired pilasters with high panelled parapet above. The entrance, in the central bay, is surmounted by a rectangular window with eared architrave and similar but taller windows occupy the adjacent bays. The interior has an end gallery supported by two fluted cast-iron columns; other contemporary fittings include – *communion table* with end drawers; *seating* in gallery; *gates* and

gate piers of cast iron in front of chapel. *Monuments*: flanking pulpit (1) Rev. John Sing, 1753, and John Sing, Gent., his son, 1810; (2) John Sing, and Sophia his wife, both 1819; in front of chapel (3) John Macmichael, 1820, Hannah, his widow, 1850, *et al.*

(6) Former CONGREGATIONAL, Stoneway Steps (SO 718930). The church formerly meeting here but since 1966 in the Wesleyan chapel, Cartway, originated in the late 17th century as a Presbyterian cause following the ejection of Rev. Andrew Tristram from the Parish Church of St Leonard. A meeting-house erected on the present site 'on the North side of the Stoneway' in 1709 was a small building with two doorways below windows in the E wall, double gables at the N and S ends, and two pillars internally to support the roof. The existing chapel was built in 1829, schoolrooms were added in 1841–2 and the chapel reseated in 1888. The building, now occupied as a theatre, has brick walls with two round-arched windows at one end flanking the site of the pulpit. The original wide entrance remains with a wooden surround having pilasters with incised key ornament and a moulded cornice. At each side of the entrance are contemporary cast-iron railings and gate piers.

Elliot (1898) 70–86.

(7) WESLEYAN, Cartway (SO 718931). Dated 1853, designed by Thomas Powell. Three-bay pedimented front of blue brick with contrasting pilasters and round-arched iron-framed windows.

BROSELEY

(8) BROSELY OLD CHAPEL (SJ 671018). The Particular Baptist church meeting here was formed in 1741 and the present chapel opened 2 February 1742. A secession led to the erection in 1803 of the Strict Baptist 'Birch Meadow' chapel which has since been closed. The Old Chapel has brick walls and a tiled roof; it was originally of three bays with an entrance in the middle bay on the N side but was extended to the W in the mid 19th century and a new entrance constructed at the E end and cast-iron frames added to the round-arched windows. The vestry and former manse adjoining to the S are approximately contemporary with the original building.

Manse and chapel from SE.

BROSELEY OLD CHAPEL, *Shropshire*

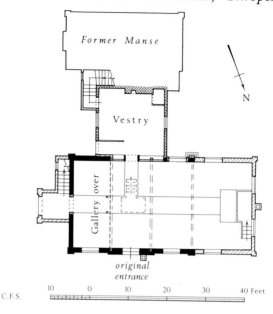

Former Manse

Vestry

Gallery over

original entrance

| 10 | 0 | 10 | 20 | 30 | 40 Feet |

C.F.S.

The interior of the chapel (22ft by 30ft enlarged to 46ft) has an early 19th-century gallery at the E end but has otherwise been refitted in the late 19th century. The roof of the older portion is supported by two collar-beam trusses with the feet of the principal rafters resting on posts embedded in the original brick-work of the walls and strengthened by curved braces at the junctions. The *vestry* wing, linking the chapel and manse, is of one storey with basement and attics. A wide outer doorway in the E wall and a wooden cross-framed window adjacent are of the mid 18th century. Two small attic rooms above the vestry, approached by a later staircase, are ceiled at collar level with bent principals below the collar. The *manse* is of two stories and attics with a three-bay elevation to the south.

Fittings – *Communion Table*: in vestry, oak with turned legs, early 18th-century. *Monuments*: in burial-ground N of chapel flanking original approach (1) John Guest, 1788, and Penelope his wife, 179[?3], brick table-tomb with stone cap, (2) Jeremiah Baker, draper, 1794, Eleanor his wife, 1804, *et al.*, double size table-tomb with cast-iron sides and stone cap, in railed enclosure, (3) George Brooks, 1777, Elizabeth his wife, 1777, *et al.*, stone table-tomb, railed, (4) Job Barker of Lightmore Iron Works, 1824, fragments of entirely cast-iron monument with pyramidal top, (5) William Roden, 1812, *et al.*, (6) Anna (Wyke) wife of Rowland Hill, 1775, *et al.*, brick table-tomb with stone cap in railed enclosure; E of vestry (7) Martha, wife of Charles Parker, 1837, brick table-tomb with cast-iron cap. *Plate*: includes a gadrooned two-handled cup of 1704, given by Dr J. W. Perrott, 1763.

(9) Former FRIENDS (SJ 67190223). A meeting-house built in 1769, superseding buildings of 1691 and 1742, was closed in 1778. From 1837 it was used as a preaching station by Independents until the erection of a chapel in 1841 when it became the

Sunday-school. Abraham Darby of Coalbrookdale was buried here, 1717. The site has now been cleared.

Elliot (1898) 251–8.

(10) WESLEYAN, Jackfield (SJ 682031). Brown brick with tiled roof. Three-bay gabled front dated 1825.

CAYNHAM

(11) WESLEYAN (SO 557735). Brick and slate with entrance in gabled end; two pointed-arched windows with wooden Y-tracery face the road. Segmental plaster ceiling. Opened 1836.

CHERRINGTON

(12) PRIMITIVE METHODIST, Tibberton (SJ 674203). Dated 1843, much altered.

CHESWARDINE

(13) WESLEYAN, Great Soudley (SJ 727288). Three-bay front with pointed-arched windows; circular tablet inscribed 'The Land graciously given by Mr John Butterton. Wesleyan Chapel Erected A.D.1837'.

CLIVE

(14) Former INDEPENDENT (SJ 517243). Yellow sandstone ashlar with a slated roof, built in 1844 replacing a chapel erected in 1830; now a workshop. Gabled to front and rear with copings and shaped kneelers. Hollow-chamfered round-arched windows at sides, altered three-bay front with date-tablet in gable.

Elliot (1898) 168–70.

(15) PRIMITIVE METHODIST (SJ 513242). Generally comparable with the foregoing but with lancet windows, 1859.

CLUNBURY

(16) PRIMITIVE METHODIST, Twitchen (SO 370793). Rubble and slate; SW front of three bays with blocked doorway between windows. Opened 1833.

CONDOVER

(17) Former CONGREGATIONAL, Dorrington (SJ 478030). Built in 1808 at the expense of Rev. William Whitfoot, Countess of Huntingdon's minister, a native of Dorrington. The chapel was pewed and a gallery added in 1822; it was enlarged at SE end in 1840 and later. Date-tablets of 1808 and 1908 in NW gable wall. *Monuments*: in burial-ground include one to Rev. John Jones Beynon, pastor, 1852, and Mary his wife, 1852, coped slab on two proto-Ionic supports. (Demolished 1973, monuments remain)

Elliot (1898) 171–6.

DAWLEY

(18) FRIENDS, Coalbrookdale (SJ 666050). Abraham Darby, who took over an existing ironworks in Coalbrookdale about 1709, gave considerable encouragement to Quaker meetings in the district and his son, also Abraham, built a meeting-house close to his works for the benefit of his workpeople, many of whom were of this persuasion. The meeting-house erected in 1745 was enlarged in 1763 and superseded by another in 1808. This was sold in 1954 and demolished *c*.1965 when a house and

shop were built on the site. The burial-ground, to the S on a steeply sloping site, is a long rectangular plot enclosed by a brick boundary wall in 1763. *Monuments*: many small rectangular stone tablets intended to lie flat but now upturned and loose against the surrounding walls, include (1) Mark Gilpin, 1799; (2) Abraham Darby, 1789; (3) Rebecca Darby, 1834; (4) Abraham Darby, 1763; (5) Abraham Darby, 1794; (6) George Titterton, 1798.

Raistrick, A., *Dynasty of Ironfounders*; *The Darbys and Coalbrookdale* (1970).

(19) WESLEYAN, High Street, Dawley (SJ 684075). Built 1860 by

Griffiths of Bridgnorth to replace a chapel of 1825. Blue brick with yellow brick dressings and slate roof. (Demolished 1977)

(20) PRIMITIVE METHODIST, Finger Road, Dawley (SJ 688069). Dated 1863. Red brick with blue brick dressings. (Demolished 1977)

(21) BAPTIST, Dawley Bank (SJ 684084). Front of blue brick with yellow brick dressings and elaborately shaped gable with

ball finials; two-storied porch added. Built 1860 on site of a chapel of 1846, date-tablet from former reset in rear wall.

(22) Former WESLEYAN, Dawley Bank (SJ 683084). Three-bay rendered front with pediment, formerly dated 1840. (Demolished 1977)

(23) WESLEYAN, Dawley Parva (SJ 683060). Three-bay front divided by pilasters, the centre bay rising through a pediment and terminating with a horizontal cornice. Dated 1837.

(24) BAPTIST, High Street, Madeley (SJ 698044). Yellow brick

and slate, three-bay front with arched centre-bay enclosing iron tablet with name ÆNON and roundel with date 1858 above.

(25) PRIMITIVE METHODIST, High Street, Madeley (SJ 700044). Yellow brick with bands of blue and dressings of blue, red and white brick. Gabled front with grouped windows and ogee hood-mould over entrance, name Mount Zion and date 1865 on gable tablet.

(26) WESLEYAN, Court Street, Madeley (SJ 696045). Dated 1841. Yellow brick with rendered dressings and slated roof.

Spacious interior with gallery around three sides supported by fluted cast-iron columns.

(27) 'ROCK CHAPEL', Madeley Wood (SJ 679034). Cottages, nos. 52 and 53 New Bridge Road, built as a single dwelling in the 17th century have been largely refaced in common brick, they were used between 1760 and 1785 by John Fletcher of Madeley as a preaching station.

(28) Former METHODIST, Madeley Wood (SJ 679035). Preaching-house erected 1777 by John Fletcher of Madeley for use as a day school and for evening worship; it was used for regular Sunday services until 1837 when superseded by a new chapel nearby (29). It has brick walls and a modern tiled roof. The gabled W front had a central round-arched doorway with small flanking windows, a tablet over without traces of inscription, and a lunette in the gable; in each side wall are three

round-arched windows with moulded stone arches, keystones and impost blocks. The interior (36ft and 24½ft) has a plaster barrel-vault of elliptical section with a moulded plaster cornice along the N and S walls; a W gallery has been removed.

(29) WESLEYAN, Madeley Wood (SJ 678036). The chapel, built in 1837 as successor to the foregoing, has walls of yellow brick; the centre bay rises through a pediment and terminates in a moulded cornice and parapet (cf (23) above).

(30) WESLEYAN, Old Park (SJ 692095). Built 1853, with lancet windows and patterned cast-iron frames; porch later. (Derelict 1980)

(31) Former PRIMITIVE METHODIST, Old Park (SJ 690096). Three-bay gabled front with two tiers of round-arched windows with iron frames; tablet with name 'Bethesda' and date 1857 above entrance. (Derelict 1973)

(32) WESLEYAN, Stirchley (SJ 694066). Low three-bay front with pediment and round-arched windows, brick surround to doorway partly covered by later porch. Built 1840–1, enlarged to rear and refitted in later 19th century.

EDGTON

(33) PRIMITIVE METHODIST (SO 387859). Rubble and slate with round-arched doorway on W side. Dated 1834; rostrum pulpit at N end.

(29) DAWLEY. Wesleyan chapel, Madeley Wood.

ELLESMERE RURAL

(34) WESLEYAN METHODIST ASSOCIATION, Dudleston Heath (SJ 365361). Brick with half-hipped slate roof, two tiers of plain pointed-arched windows in W wall and side-entry porch with tablet inscribed 'EBENE'ZER/CHAPEL.A.D.1835./STAND fast therefore in the *liberty* wherewith Christ hath/made us *free*, and be not/entangled again with the *yoke*/of *bondage*. Gal.V. & I.'. Brick bell-cote and weathervane at N end.

(35) CONGREGATIONAL, Frankton (SJ 366331). Rubble with brick dressings to round-arched windows. Built 1834, refitted 1877. (URC)
    Elliot (1898) 238–9.

ERCALL MAGNA

(36) WESLEYAN, Ellerdine Heath (SJ 618219). Opened 1813.

FARLOW

(37) WESLEYAN (SO 644798). Rubble and slate, gabled front with a tablet inscribed 'MELVILLE/CHAPEL/EBENEZER PLACE/1833'.

GREAT NESS

(38) CONGREGATIONAL, Wilcott (SJ 374192). Built in 1834; walls of large blocks of sandstone rubble and a slated roof gabled

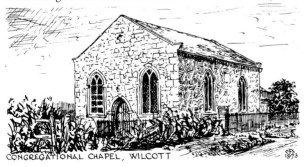

CONGREGATIONAL CHAPEL, WILCOTT

to N and S with shaped kneelers. The entrance is at the S end. *Monument*: Mary, widow of Richard Jones of Oswestry, 1852 and their daughters Elizabeth, 1857, 'more than 24 years nurse in the family of John Horatio Lloyd, Barrister at Law, London', and Susan, 1858, table-tomb. (URC)
    Elliot (1898) 243–6.

HADNALL

(39) Former PRIMITIVE METHODIST (SJ 521197). Red brick with stone dressings and a tiled roof. E front of three bays, with

PRIMITIVE METHODIST CHAPEL, HADNALL

brick pilasters rising to simple stone pinnacles, gablet between centre pair with defaced date-tablet of 1862.

(40) Former PRIMITIVE METHODIST, Yorton Heath (SJ 504223). Dated 1859.

HINSTOCK

(41) WESLEYAN (SJ 692269). Opened 1831. Squared sandstone walls with trefoiled window over later N porch and three round-arched windows on E side.

HODNET

(42) CONGREGATIONAL, Wollerton (SJ 620304). Wheel window: 1867–8 by Thomas Huxley of Malpas. (URC)
    CYB (1869) 323–4; Elliot (1898) 156–61.

(43) Former PRIMITIVE METHODIST, Kenstone (SJ 596287). Brick and tile with three-bay front and round-arched windows; mid 19th-century.

HOPESAY

(44) BAPTIST, Aston on Clun (SO 394818). Rubble and slate, three-bay gabled front with rectangular labels over windows and tablet inscribed 'BAPTIST/CHAPEL, 1844/PREPARE TO/MEET THY GOD.' Pulpit opposite entrance has two turned wood candle-sticks on front corners.

(45) Former PRIMITIVE METHODIST, Aston on Clun (SO 395819). Dated 1862.

KINNERLEY

(46) BAPTIST, Maesbrook Green (SJ 304212). 'ÆNON CHAPEL', dated 1844, has red brick walls with stone dressings and a slated roof. Three-bay gabled front with shaped kneelers and lancet windows.

(47) PRIMITIVE METHODIST, Maesbrook (SJ 310214). The former chapel of 1844 stands at right angles to its successor built 1899. Brick and slate with pointed-arched windows.

LILLESHALL

(48) Former BAPTIST, Queens Road, Donnington Wood (SJ 710133). Tablet in gable 'BAPTIST CHAPEL/ESTABLISHED 1820/RESTORED 1906'. Now a builder's store.

LUDLOW

(49) Former CHAPEL, Corve Street (SO 511753). A former dissenters' meeting-house erected in 1736 behind houses on the W side of Corve Street was demolished *c*.1960. It was built, following disturbed meetings in a private house, by a congregation which appears to have had slender denominational attachments. About 1800 the church was re-formed as Independent, removing in 1830 to a new chapel in Old Street (see (50) below). Some use by other denominations, including Moravians, has also been claimed and in 1889 Congregational services were resumed.

The chapel (44¾ft by 17ft externally), of which only some foundations remain, had brick walls and a tiled roof. It was gabled to E and W with an entrance below the E window removed to the S side *c*.1876. The pulpit in front of the W window with its sounding-board and a complete set of box-pews were still in position in 1951.

Elliot (1898) 97–105: England (1886) I, 5, pl.8.

(50) Former CONGREGATIONAL, Old Street (SO 513746). The chapel, built in 1830 by a congregation which removed from Corve Street (see (49) above), was closed *c*.1968 and has since been converted to a house. It stands on a restricted site behind

houses on the W side of the street. The walls are of brick and the pedimented front has the date of erection displayed in large raised numerals below the apex. A single end-gallery of later date was approached by a staircase covering part of the frontage.

Plate: includes two gadrooned two-handled cups: of 1703, given by Mary Reed, 1744; of 1768, given by James Hockey, 1859.

Elliot (1898) 97–105.

MARKET DRAYTON

(51) Former CONGREGATIONAL, Church Lane (SJ 67553405). Although the vicar was amongst those ejected for non-conformity in 1662 no continuous thread of dissent can be established. Meetings of Independents commenced about 1768, a church was formed in 1776 and the meeting-house erected two years later, the builder being William Griffith. A gallery was added *c*.1841–7 and substantial additions were made to the rear in 1865–7. In 1895 the chapel was drastically altered internally by the insertion of a floor at gallery level and the conversion of the lower part to classrooms. The chapel was closed by 1949 and has since been used for a variety of purposes.

The walls are of red brick and the roof is hipped and covered with tiles. The broad SE front has a brick dentil eaves cornice and a central entrance from which a wooden doorcase has been

removed. Above the doorway is an oval tablet dated 1778. The late 19th-century enlargement to the rear has two tiers of round-arched windows and a triple gable to the north.

The interior (34ft by 44ft) has a flat plaster ceiling and original moulded cornice. Before subdivision the gallery stairs were in the front corners approached directly by doorways inserted in place of windows in the side walls. The basic structure of the mid 19th-century gallery remains, supported by cast-iron columns of quatrefoil section; short lengths of the panelled gallery-fronts also survive. In the late 19th century the NW wall was pierced at gallery level to provide an organ-chamber and choir gallery behind the pulpit, the walling above being supported by two cast-iron columns and half-columns with Corinthian capitals, by Barwell & Co., Northampton. When a floor was inserted at gallery level a new staircase was built opposite the front entrance and the former staircases removed.

The roof is supported by two main trusses with king-posts, queen-posts and diagonal struts; there is no ridge-piece. A half-

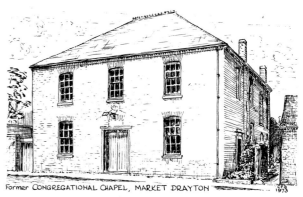

Former CONGREGATIONAL CHAPEL, MARKET DRAYTON   1973

Former Congregational Chapel, Church Lane
MARKET DRAYTON
Shropshire

N

5 Feet 0   5   10   15   20

truss on the principal axis supported a central chandelier for which a large stone counterweight remains.

Inscriptions: painted on roof timbers, 'Wm: Griffith 1778 Fecit'; 'Thomas Tuker 1778'; 'Isaac Griffith & Thos Corfield repaired this Ceiling Novr. 2 1832'. *Monument*: in yard SW of chapel, to William Griffith, 1822, 'he erected this Chapel in the year 1778 and filled the office of Deacon until his death', Elizabeth his wife, 1814, and John his brother, 1805, deacon.

Elliot (1898) 115–24.

(52) WESLEYAN, Shrewsbury Road (SJ 671340). Red brick with stone dressings, broach spire at corner carried by dwarf columns; by G. Bidlake, 1864.

(53) PRIMITIVE METHODIST, Frogmore Road (SJ 674341). Red brick with blue brick dressings and slate roof, round-arched windows, corner pilasters carried up to simple stone pinnacles (see (39) above). Tablet in front gable 'Ebenezer . . . 1867'.

MELVERLEY

(54) Former CONGREGATIONAL, Cross Lanes (SJ 331183). Built 1842–5. Converted to a cottage and refenestrated.

Elliot (1898) 265–7.

(55) PRIMITIVE METHODIST, Cross Lanes (SJ 329182). Dated 1865. Red brick with yellow brick dressings and slate roof.

MINSTERLEY

(56) CONGREGATIONAL (SJ 375050). Baptists and Independents commenced joint meetings in the late 18th century forming a

united church in 1805. In 1833 the two groups separated, the former building a chapel 'close to Snailbeach Mines' (see (116) below) and the latter erecting the present building. The chapel has brick walls, now rendered, and a slated roof, two tiers of round-arched windows with iron frames, a gabled front from which a parapet has been removed, and a gabled porch of two stories. Date 1833 in front wall.

Elliot (1898) 137–40.

MUCH WENLOCK

(57) Former WESLEYAN, Shineton Street (SJ 623001). The chapel, which stands well back on the W side of the street, was built *c*.1830; it is now in commercial use. Rubble walls with brick dressings and a hipped tiled roof. The E front, now rebuilt, had a small porch between pointed-arched windows; the side walls have brick dentil eaves cornices and original round-arched windows with iron frames.

(58) PRIMITIVE METHODIST, King Street (SO 622999). Brown brick with dressings of blue and white brick, gabled front dated 1862; 'Sabbath-school' in similar style adjacent to left, 1883.

MYDDLE

(59) Former INDEPENDENT, Harmer Hill (SJ 489226). The chapel, built 1833–4 as the result of successful preaching by Rev.

George Rogers of Bomere Heath (see (75) below), was transferred in 1920 to the Calvinistic Methodists (Presbyterian Church of Wales) who still use it. The walls are built of large squared blocks of red sandstone and the roof is hipped and slate covered. The S wall has a porch with two crude stone columns supporting a segmental-pointed arch; a tablet above the entrance is inscribed 'INDEPENDENT CHAPEL 1833'. The E and W walls originally had two windows but a third was added to each side when a minor room to the N was incorporated into the chapel. The manse adjacent to the N has been enlarged. *Monuments*: W of chapel, three mid 19th-century table-tombs, including one to Elizabeth Wilkinson Rogers, 1841.

Elliot (1898) 240–2.

NEWPORT

(60) CONGREGATIONAL, Wellington Road (SJ 746187). The chapel, built in 1832, has brick walls rendered at the front in

(62) OAKENGATES. Congregational chapel. (URC)

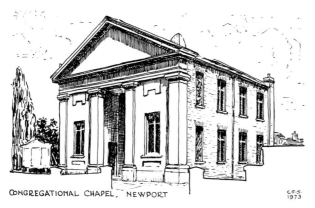

CONGREGATIONAL CHAPEL, NEWPORT   C.F.S. 1973

stucco. The front has an open bay at the centre to form a porch with doorways in the return walls. The interior was refurbished in the late 19th century but retains an original gallery supported by thin iron columns. *Fontlet*: pottery, Winchester type, with pyramidal cover. (URC)

Elliot (1898) 106–14.

(61) Former PRIMITIVE METHODIST, Wellington Road (SJ 746188). Red brick with yellow brick dressings and tiled roof. Three-bay gabled front with arched centre bay (*cf* (58) above) date-tablet of 1866, now defaced.

OAKENGATES

(62) CONGREGATIONAL, Lion Street (SJ 696109). Brown brick and slate. pedimented front; four-bay sides with fifth bay of two stories added at rear. Built 1847–8; side galleries inserted after 1857. (URC)

Elliot (1898) 275–8.

(63) UNITED METHODIST FREE CHURCHES, New Street (SJ 703110). Three-bay pedimented front; tablet inscribed 'METHODIST FREE CHURCH 1855'. (Derelict)

(64) WESLEYAN, Ketleybank (SJ 694103). Three-bay pedimented front with later porch. Dated 1823.

(65) PRIMITIVE METHODIST, Ketleybank (SJ 691103). Built 1859; enlarged and refronted 1907.

(66) PRIMITIVE METHODIST, Station Hill (SJ 699110). Brown brick with blue brick dressings and slate roof, 'erected 1847 rebuilt 1868'.

OSWESTRY

(67) Former CONGREGATIONAL, Arthur Street (SJ 28982978). The congregation, which for a period prior to *c*.1777 was regarded as Presbyterian, originated in the mid 17th century and is said to have met from 1651 at Sweeney (2 miles S) having a burial ground near Sweeney Hall, and to have built a meeting-house in Oswestry in 1659. The site in Arthur Street, described as 'a Building and Malt Mill, lying in Oswestry near the Castle Hill . . .', was acquired in 1748 and a new meeting-house erected thereon was opened in 1750; this was several times enlarged and in 1830 replaced by the present building which served the church until 1872 (see (68) below) being then converted for use as a Sunday-school. It is now in commercial occupation.

The chapel has brick walls with two tiers of round-arched windows, three-bay front with heightened and rebuilt gable, central doorway and porch with two fluted Doric columns *in antis*. *Burial-ground*: at side of chapel, now derelict.

Elliot (1898) 29–46.

(68) CONGREGATIONAL (SJ 290298). 'Christ Church', 50 yards NE of the foregoing, was built 1871–2 on the site of the Borough Gaol to designs in the Gothic style by W. H. Spaull of Oswestry. It has stone walls and a corner tower with broach spire. (URC)

CYB (1873) 428: Elliot (1898) 29–46.

OSWESTRY RURAL

(69) BAPTIST, Sweeney (SJ 284260). Rubble and slate, three windows and doorway in front wall all with two-centred arched heads, built *c*.1831 but woodwork renewed in late 19th century.

(70) CONGREGATIONAL, Maesbury Marsh (SJ 312252). Brick with stone dressings and slate roof, corner spire supported by dwarf columns (*cf* (52) above), 1868 by W. H. Spaull of

CONGREGATIONAL CHAPELS, MAESBURY MARSH

Oswestry. Former chapel adjacent with two pointed-arched windows in brick gabled front dated 1855. (URC)
CYB (1870) 381: Elliot (1898) 47–50.

(71) CONGREGATIONAL, Trefonen (SJ 259269). Rubble walls and a modern tiled roof. The E wall has three pointed-arched windows and a stone tablet above the entrance apparently inscribed 'CARNEDAU INDEPENDENT CHAPEL . . .' but largely concealed by the roof of a later porch. Built 1834.
Elliot (1898) 50–4.

(72) PRIMITIVE METHODIST, Ball (SJ 306266). 'Bethesda Chapel', dated 1834, of rubble and slate. Windows have pointed-arched heads.

(73) PRIMITIVE METHODIST, Morton (SJ 290240). 'Bethel Chapel', dated 1838, of rubble and slate with later porch.

(74) PRIMITIVE METHODIST, Treflach Wood (SJ 260252). Dated 1833.

PIMHILL

(75) Former CONGREGATIONAL, Bomere Heath (SJ 474197). The chapel, built in 1827, has been used since c.1879 by Calvinistic Methodists. The walls are of red sandstone in large squared blocks and the roof is covered with small slates. The entrance at the E end of the N wall is covered by a later stone porch and has above it the mis-spelt tablet 'ZION'S HIIL 1827'. The windows have been much altered; two windows in the N wall formerly had stone lintels and external shutters, and a large

E window replaces a much smaller circular light. Two-storied vestry wing at W end. *Monuments*: in burial ground (1) Mrs Mary Ash, 1841 and Mrs Rachel Ash, 1844, (2) Elizabeth Hill, 1843, (3) Rev. George Rogers, minister of Bomere Heath and Harmer Hill, 1868, also Annie Hickson Rogers. (*cf* (59) above).
CYB (1869) 274: Elliot (1898) 208–12.

(76) WESLEYAN, Bomere Heath (SJ 473198). Alongside the red brick chapel of 1903 stands the smaller former chapel with walls of squared red sandstone blocks and a tiled roof. Although

inscribed ' . . . erected 1836 rebuilt 1868' the building is of the former date and prior to drastic refitting had an entrance in the front gabled wall and three windows with round-arched heads at the sides.

PONTESBURY

(77) BAPTIST, Chapel Street (SJ 401060). Built c.1828 for a church founded in that year. Rendered walls and tiled roof; two round-arched windows in the front wall, entrance perhaps formerly between.

(78) PLEALEY CHAPEL (SJ 423070) was built in the early 19th century on the estate and at the expense of 'a gentleman who resided in the neighbourhood' who at first supported the Independents but later, c.1839, transferred his allegiance and the chapel to the Baptists and again, c.1858, to the Wesleyan Methodists who still use it. Brick walls and slate roof with small

PLEALEY CHAPEL, PONTESBURY

porch at one end. *Monument*: in yard at rear, to Richard France, 1829, Richard France, 1862, Hannah, his widow, 1866, *et al.*, table-tomb.

Elliot (1898) 140.

(79) CONGREGATIONAL (SJ 397062). Independents deprived of the use of Plealey Chapel (78) erected a new chapel in 1839. This has rendered walls and a slate roof. It forms part of a continuous range with the chapel at the centre, manse at the W and two-

storied Sunday-school to the east. Two tall round-arched windows in the S wall and two in the N light the chapel; a third window beyond the S porch is bisected by the upper floor of the Sunday-school. Interior refitted 1871.

Elliot (1898) 137–43.

(80) PRIMITIVE METHODIST, Asterley (SJ 375071). Dated 1834. Sandstone rubble with brick eaves-cornice and slate roof. Gabled front with two round-arched windows with iron frames and mean later porch. Interior has open-backed benches, rostrum pulpit, and rows of hat pegs.

(81) PRIMITIVE METHODIST, Pontesbury Hill Road (SJ 398058). Opened 1845. Rendered three-bay front. Original open-backed benches.

PREES

(82) WESLEYAN, Darliston (SJ 581335). The chapel, designed by William Smith of Whitchurch and built by John Powell of

Wesleyan Chapel, Darliston, PREES, *Shropshire*

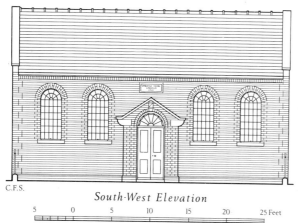

C.F.S.

South-West Elevation

5　0　5　10　15　20　25 Feet

Darliston, has walls of red brick with dressings of blue and yellow bricks used alternately in the eaves-cornice, the doorway and window surrounds, and as quoins at the ends of the front elevation; the roof is covered with slates. The windows have cast-iron frames, and above the porch is a tablet inscribed 'WESLEYAN CHAPEL/ERECTED/1861'.

RODINGTON

(83) PRIMITIVE METHODIST, Marsh Green (SJ 608142). Dated 1841.

(84) WESLEYAN, Rodington (SJ 582141). Dated 1834; enlarged to E in late 19th century.

RUYTON-XI-TOWNS

(85) CONGREGATIONAL (SJ 392228). The chapel, erected 1833, stands N of the village close to the S entrance to Ruyton Park. The builder was Nathanael Edwards of Ruyton. It has walls of yellow sandstone rubble with ashlar dressings and a slate roof,

pointed-arched windows and buttresses originally intended to terminate in pinnacles. (URC)

Elliot (1898) 227–37.

ST MARTIN'S

(86) PRIMITIVE METHODIST, St Martin's Moor (SJ 315358). Red brick with polychrome dressings, steeply-gabled porch with tablet inscribed '. . . built 1829 rebuilt 1870'.

SHAWBURY

(87) WESLEYAN, Moretonmill (SJ 577226). Alongside the red-brick chapel of 1875 stands its smaller predecessor, of brick and slate with tablet dated 1846 in the front gable and pointed-arched windows with intersecting glazing bars in the side walls.

SHREWSBURY

(88) HIGH STREET CHAPEL (SJ 492124). The Presbyterian congregation, in existence by 1673, traces its origins to the two ejected ministers Rev. Francis Tallents, vicar of St Mary's, and Rev. John Bryan, vicar of St Chad's. Prior to 1690 meetings were held in the house of Mrs Hunt, widow of one of the members of the Long Parliament, and afterwards in the house of Francis Tallents until the completion of the first meeting-house

on the present site, then known as Bakers Row, in October 1691. This survived until 6 July 1715 when it was destroyed by a mob and subsequently rebuilt at the public expense. On the appointment of Job Orton as minister in 1741 the congregation was joined by a large personal following of Independents to form a joint church which then preferred the designation 'Christian'; in 1766 a doctrinal dispute over the appointment of a minister resulted in the withdrawal of the orthodox members to re-form the Independent meeting which then gathered at Swan Hill (see (89) below); the remaining 'Presbyterian' members gradually adopted a liberal system of theology and now support a Unitarian ministry. In 1839–40 the meeting-house was almost entirely rebuilt in consequence of its poor structural condition and the requirement of part of the site for street improvement; an addition to the front of the chapel was made in 1885.

The chapel stands on a restricted site on the SW side of the street, in 1691 it measured 50ft 2in. deep and from 27ft 7in. to 29ft 2in. in width. The walls are of brick and the front is faced in ashlar. The front wall, of 1885, is of three bays with tall pilasters, central entrance and round-arched upper windows. The side walls, not visible externally, are each pierced at a high level by a rectangular window of three lights and by a smaller window at each end; the end wall is blank. Behind the forebuilding, which provides on the ground floor an entrance lobby, vestry and staircase and a large meeting-room above, the chapel (56ft by 24½ft) is of irregular shape with a gallery at the NE end having a bolection-moulded panelled front of the early 18th century supported by two square fluted wooden posts; the pews were reconstructed in 1905.

Fittings – *Clock*: on gallery front, dated 1724. *Communion Table*: with turned baluster legs, 18th-century. *Glass*: in side windows, double-glazed *c*.1839. *Monuments* include one to Charles Darwin, 1882, a native of Shrewsbury, and a brass tablet to Samuel Coleridge who preached here in 1798 with a view to the pastorate (see William Hazlitt's essay 'My first acquaintance with Poets'). *Plate* includes a pair of tall cups of 1736 given by John Bryan. *Panelling*: on SW wall, early 18th-century. *Royal Arms*: on SW wall, Hanoverian 1714–1800, large framed panel. *Seating*: chairs, pair, with tall panelled backs, 18th-century.

Broadbent, A., *The Story of Unitarianism in Shrewsbury* (1962): Evans (1897) 223–5: Evans (1899) 181–93: Reavley (1925).

(89) SWAN HILL CHAPEL (SJ 489123). A society of Independents is believed to have met prior to 1662 in a house in the King's Head Shut or Peacock Shut. This united with the Presbyterian congregation in 1741 (see (88) above). In 1766, following the resignation of the minister, Job Orton, and on his advice, a separate Independent meeting was recommenced and a meeting-house erected on the present site in Swan Hill in the following year. This had brick walls and a hipped roof, with a two-stage front of three bays having round-arched doorways with pedimental surrounds in the end bays and three round-arched windows with triple keystones and imposts to the upper stage. In 1868 the chapel was rebuilt to a larger size by George Bidlake of Wolverhampton incorporating parts of the side walls of the former building; schoolrooms were added in 1880.

The lower part of the SW wall, dating from 1767, is of brick

having two blind windows with flat-arched heads and triple keystones; the upper part has been rebuilt. The NE wall is covered by later building. The present chapel, of brick with stone dressings, has a gabled front to the SE with a four-light window above the entrance with plate tracery in a two-centred head. The interior (38ft wide, being the maximum dimension of the former meeting-house) is divided into nave and aisles by arcades of four bays with cast-iron columns supporting two-centred arches with a clerestory over, and has a gallery around three sides.

Fittings – *Chair*: in front of pulpit, with round-arched back panel inscribed 'S 1611 P'. *Monuments*: pair in chapel to Rev. Thomas Weaver, 1852, and Mary his wife, 1838; in forecourt late 18th-century ledger-stones. *Paintings*: (1) Rev. Richard Heath, died *c*.1666; (2) Rev. James Owen, 1654–1706; (3) Rev. Francis Tallents, 1619–1708, dated 1704; (4) Rev. Job Orton, 1717–83; (5) Rev. Samuel Lucas, *c*.1748–99. *Plate* includes two cups of 1778.

CYB (1868) 335: Barker [*c*.1910] 18–24: Elliot (1898) 14–28.

(90) BAPTIST, Claremont (SJ 490125). The church seems to have originated in the late 17th century; a meeting-house was built 1735 in Stilliards Shutt whence the congregation removed to the

present site, then named Dog Lane, in 1780. The chapel, rebuilt 1877–8, is of brick with stone dressings, the centre bay having a pediment supported by paired Corinthian pilasters and with open balustrades with urns above the flanking bays. A few decayed grave-slabs of the early 19th century remain in the forecourt.

Barker [*c*.1910] 24–5.

(91) CONGREGATIONAL, Abbey Foregate (SJ 497124). Stone and slate, in geometrical Gothic style with corner tower and banded stone spire, by George Bidlake of Wolverhampton. Built for a newly-formed congregation in 1863 as a bicentenary memorial. (URC)

CYB (1864) 289: Elliot (1898) 294–302.

(92) THE TABERNACLE, Dogpole (SJ 493125). Three-bay Italianate front of ashlar; bicentenary memorial chapel built 1862, architect Rev. T. Thomas of Swansea, for a Welsh Independent church formerly meeting in a chapel on Pride Hill.

CYB (1862) 317: Elliot (1898) 259–64.

(93) Former FRIENDS, St John's Hill (SJ 48851240). The meeting-house, rebuilt c.1807, stands 50 yards E of St Chad's church behind 24 St John's Hill, a house of brick and tile with two stories and attics contemporary with the original building of 1746. After Friends use ceased prior to 1863 it was used by seceders from the Baptists in Claremont and subsequently as an office for the Board of Guardians; it is now used in part as a Kingdom Hall of the Jehovah's Witnesses. The entrance from the street is through a semicircular archway with triple keystone and imposts and double doors. The meeting-house has brick walls and a slate-covered roof, the E and W walls have pedimented gables and in the N and S walls are three flat-arched windows with hung sashes; traces of a former porch remain on the S side. The interior, formerly divided into two rooms, has an original moulded plaster ceiling cornice.

Barker [c.1910] 27.

(94) WESLEYAN, St John's Hill (SJ 489124). Methodist preaching commenced in 1761 with the visit of John Wesley. Twenty years later a preaching-house was erected in Hills Lane by John Appleton at his own expense and in 1804–5 a new chapel was built on the present site. The chapel, rebuilt in 1879, of red brick with stone dressings, has a front of five bays with a pediment, central entrance and round-arched windows.

Barker [c.1910] 33–49.

(95) Former METHODIST NEW CONNEXION, Town Walls (SJ 491122). 'Ebenezer Chapel', built in 1834 for a cause founded in the previous year, has walls of brick, rendered at the front and sides in stucco, and stands above basement rooms. The front is of five bays with Corinthian pilasters and porches with fluted Doric columns. (Under conversion to secular use 1983)

Barker [c.1910] fig. 54, 64.

(96) PRESBYTERIAN, Castle Street (SJ 494127). A congregation of the Presbyterian Church in England was formed in 1865 as a preaching station of the Lancashire Presbytery and first met in the Music Hall. The present building, which stands on the site of the mediaeval chapel of St Nicholas, was built in 1870 to designs

by Robert C. Bennett of Weymouth. It is a tall building in the Romanesque style with stone walls and a tiled roof. The SW front has a wide arched entrance of three orders flanked by pilaster buttresses and a circular staircase tower at the W corner. There are minor rooms on the ground floor below the chapel. (Closed 1975 and congregation united with (91))

Reavley (1925).

STANTON LACY

(97) WESLEYAN, Hayton's Bent (SO 518805). Rubble walls and tiled roof. Opened 1838.

(98) Former PRIMITIVE METHODIST, Upper Hayton (SO 518809). Rubble with polychrome brick dressings; tiled roof. Gabled S front with tablet dated 1877.

STOKE UPON TERN

(99) Former CONGREGATIONAL, Ollerton (SJ 650253). Built 1838. Walls of squared red sandstone blocks and hipped slated roof. Entrance at E end and external stone staircase to E gallery. Pointed-arched windows in N and S walls.

Elliot (1898) 180–2.

(100) CONGREGATIONAL, Wistanwick (SJ 668288). The chapel, built about 1805 by Rev. John Wilson of Market Drayton at his own expense, was put in trust in 1833, enlarged between 1859 and 1864 and a manse was added in 1873. The walls are of squared red sandstone blocks and the roofs are tiled. The S half of

CONGREGATIONAL CHAPEL, WISTANWICK

the chapel appears to date from c.1805, and has a gable to the E and traces of a former doorway in the S wall; when the chapel was enlarged to the N the fenestration was made uniform throughout with three round-arched windows to N and S and two entrances covered by low gabled porches were made in the extended double-gabled E wall. The manse, a small two-storied cottage, is attached to the west. (URC)

Elliot (1898) 177–80.

(101) PRIMITIVE METHODIST, Stoke Heath (SJ 647294). Built 1841; former three-bay front extended to left and heightened.

STOTTESDON

(102) WESLEYAN (SO 670829). Rendered rubble and slate. Gabled front dated 1849. Small rear gallery with plain balus-traded front; open-backed benches with shaped ends.

TELFORD (For monuments within the boundaries of the new town see: DAWLEY, LILLESHALL, OAKENGATES, WELLINGTON RURAL, WELLINGTON URBAN)

WELLINGTON RURAL

(103) Former WESLEYAN REFORM, Ketley (SJ 680110). On N side of Watling Street. Brick and slate; pedimented S front with terminal pilasters; dated 1852.

WELLINGTON URBAN

(104) Former BAPTIST, King Street, Wellington (SJ 652119). Built in the early 19th century for a church formed in 1807. Square, with brick walls in three bays and two tiers of round-arched windows. (Derelict 1973)

WELSHAMPTON

(105) PRIMITIVE METHODIST, Breaden Heath (SJ 447364). Brick and slate, three-bay front dated 1832; contemporary cottage adjacent.

(106) PRIMITIVE METHODIST, Welshampton (SJ 438351). 1843.

WEM RURAL

(107) PRIMITIVE METHODIST, Northwood (SJ 466333). Brick and slate 'Jubilee Chapel' dated 1860, 'The land kindly given by W. Williams'. Front with patterned cast-iron window frames.

WEM URBAN

(108) Former PRESBYTERIAN, Noble Street, Wem (SJ 512289). A Presbyterian congregation met in a converted barn in Leek Lane (Chapel Street) in the late 17th century; the building was destroyed by a mob in 1715 and a new site, 'Sarah Thornhill's garden in Noble Street', was acquired and a meeting-house built there the following year. Between 1755 and 1817 heterodox preachers filled the pulpit but in the later 19th century the orthodox party appears to have prevailed and in 1874 when the chapel closed the remaining members joined the church meeting in Chapel Street (see (109) below). William Hazlitt, the father of the essayist, was minister here 1788–1813 and is commemorated by a modern tablet on the wall of the former manse, 17 Noble Street, adjacent to the chapel.

Former Presbyterian Chapel, WEM, *Shropshire*

former doorway

The former chapel of 1716, standing on the S side of the street at the back of the White Horse p.h. in High Street, has been drastically altered and reduced in height for use as a garage. It has walls of brown brick with dressings of yellow sandstone; the roof was formerly tiled. The walls rise from a moulded stone plinth and have rusticated quoins and a plain stone platband above mid-height. The original entrance at the N end, now blocked, has a stone lintel and jambs; traces of three upper windows are visible, one with a pointed-arched head. Two closely-set windows in the S wall flanking the site of the pulpit and three windows in the E wall, apparently repeated in the W wall but now altered by the insertion of garage doors, all have pointed-arched heads. The interior (40¼ft by 20½ft) retains no original features. Fittings now dispersed included two mid 18th-century communion cups and a large library presented in 1730. Elliot (1898) 60–6: Evans (1897) 252–3.

(109) INDEPENDENT, Chapel Street, Wem (SJ 513288). The congregation originated with meetings held at the house of John Henshaw who enlisted the assistance of students from Trevecka, built the chapel in 1775 at his own cost next to his house and placed it at the disposal of the Countess of Huntingdon's Connexion. The patronage was subsequently returned to the donor the cause becoming fully Independent about 1792 (now URC). In 1834 the chapel was drastically enlarged; it was further altered, refitted, and an organ chamber erected after 1873.

The chapel has brick walls faced at the front with yellow sandstone ashlar and the roof is covered with slates. The E front, probably of 1834, is of three bays with a pediment and terminal pilasters. Brickwork of 1775 remains visible in the side walls with a round-arched window with keystone at the former centre of the S wall; the chapel has been extended to the west. The interior (originally 26ft by 40¾ft, the former increased to 46¼ft in 1834) has an E gallery of the early 19th century now approached from the S by a staircase wing added post 1873; the walls are divided by pilasters carrying a Doric entablature with a semicircular organ-arch on the W side behind the rostrum.

Monuments: in chapel (1) John Henshaw Esq., attorney, 1801

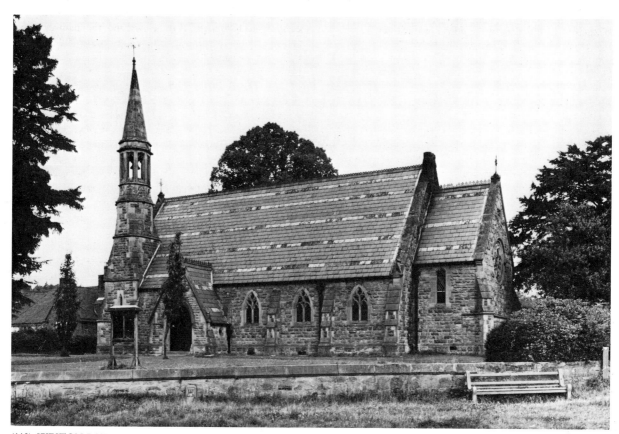

(110) WESTON RHYN. Congregational chapel, The Quinta. (URC)

(113) WHITCHURCH URBAN. Former Presbyterian meeting-house from W.

'...this edifice having been erected and endowed at his sole expence...' and Jane (Tippet) his wife, 1800, marble tablet with wreath, signed Bacon, London, S. Manning Ft; in burial-ground on E side of road opposite chapel; (2) Rev. W. Jones, 1852, [Baptist] 'minister of the gospel in this town'.

Elliot (1898) 59, 66–9: Seymour II (1839) 39–40.

WESTON RHYN

(110) CONGREGATIONAL, The Quinta (SJ 281360). The chapel was built in 1858 by Thomas Barnes, Liberal M.P. for Bolton 1852–7 and 1861–8, who had recently acquired and rebuilt a house at the Quinta. A church (now URC) was formed in 1862. Stone and slate in the Gothic style comprising a short chancel, nave of six bays, S porch and SW turret. The E window of the chancel is circular, the N and S windows of the nave are of two lights with tracery in two-centred arched heads, and the S porch has a pointed-arched outer doorway with decorative wrought-iron grilles. The SW turret rises to an octagonal belfry with one bell and has a short spire.

Elliot (1898) 280–8.

(111) Former WESLEYAN, Weston Rhyn (SJ 287359). Dated 1849. Yellow sandstone rubble with segmental-arched doorway and two pointed-arched windows in side walls.

(112) PRIMITIVE METHODIST, Pontfaen (SJ 279369). Rubble and slate, three-bay front dated 1839.

WHITCHURCH URBAN

(113) Former PRESBYTERIAN, Dodington, Whitchurch (SJ 54254130). The congregation formerly meeting here is believed to have originated in the late 17th century partly through the ministrations of Philip Henry, father of the commentator Matthew Henry, who was ejected in 1662 from Worthenbury, Flintshire, and in 1672 licensed his house at Broad Oak in the

same county (3 miles W of Whitchurch). A meeting-house at Broad Oak was registered in 1689 and superseded by one in Whitchurch built in 1707; the latter was destroyed by a mob in 1715 and replaced in the following year by the present building, the former meeting-house at Broad Oak perhaps serving meanwhile as temporary accommodation (a baptism is recorded at Broad Oak, 3 September 1715 'the chappel at Whitchurch being demolished by ye mobb on July 15th, 16th, 18th and 19th, before'). The meeting suffered severely from an orthodox secession in 1798 (see (114) below) and the remnant who countenanced a more liberal theology disbanded in 1844. The building subsequently served as a British School, a dance hall, and is now a builder's store.

The meeting-house stands on a confined site behind buildings on the SW side of Dodington. It has brick walls and a hipped tiled roof with gablets to NW and SE. The front wall is rendered and has a moulded stone plinth and rusticated quoins, the doorway, left of centre, and two segmental-arched windows have been altered in the 19th century; two windows in the rear wall, formerly with round-arched heads, flank the probable site of the pulpit. The NW end wall has been much rebuilt and the SE wall was removed in the 19th century when the building was extended by 12ft at this end. The interior (originally $27\frac{3}{4}$ft by $40\frac{1}{2}$ft) has a plaster ceiling with a wide cove along each side. No traces of galleries or other fittings remain.

Brasses: a series of twenty-three memorial tablets was rediscovered by George Eyre Evans concealed behind wall panelling and removed in 1896 to the Church of the Saviour, Whitchurch, of which he was then minister. The tablets, now in the care of the Congregational (United Reformed) Church (items 5 and 15 missing), are fully described in Evans (1899), 241–5. (1) Samuel Benyon, 1791, and Lydia his widow, 1801, with shield-of-arms, signed W. Bowley, Engraver, Shrewsbury; (2) Mary Benyon, 1765; (3) Elizabeth, wife of Benjamin Benyon, 1797, with shield-of-arms; (4) Elizabeth, wife of S.Y. Benyon, 1802, with shield-of-arms; [(5) Samuel Yate Benyon K.C., 1822, Vice Chancellor of the Duchy of Lancaster, Attorney General and Recorder of Chester, with shield-of-arms]; (6) Constance Benyon, second wife of S.Y. Benyon, 1836, with shield-of-arms; (7) Lydia Collyer, 1744; (8) Edward Edwards, 1785, and Mary his widow, 1802; (9) John Edwards, 1825, and William his son, 1825; (10) John Edwards, 1827, and Margaret his widow, 1832; (11) Robert Gentleman, 1757, and his daughters Sarah and Martha (12) John Holt, 1781, and Ann his widow, 1782, with remains of earlier inscription on back to Thomas Keay, 17[80] (see (15) below); (13) Rev. 'Ebeneezer' Keay, 1779, 40 years minister of this place; (14) Hannah, wife of Rev. Ebenezer Keay, 1766; [(15) Thomas Keay, 1780, and Lydia his widow, 1785, with shield-of-arms] (16) Thomas Yate Keay, 1826, with shield-of-arms; (17) Thomas Yate, 1746, Elizabeth his wife, 1756, their sons Thomas and Collyer and daughters Susannah, and Anna, 1754, with cartouche-of-arms; (18) Samuel, son of Thomas Yate, 1729, and Abigail his daughter,

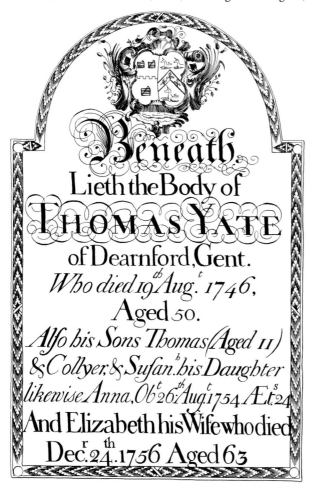

widow of Edward Ellis, 1746; (19) Benjamin Yate, 1756, with cartouche-of-arms; (20) Elizabeth Yate, 1767; (21) Thomas Yate, 1765, and Lydia his wife, 1757, with cartouche-of-arms; (22) John Yate, 1780, and Constance his widow, 1787, with shield-of-arms; (23) Constance Mary Yate, 1762, Anna Yate, 1762, and Margaret Yate, 1769, with cartouche-of-arms.

Elliot (1898) 88–90: Evans (1897) 255–7: Evans (1899) 240–8.

(114) CONGREGATIONAL, Dodington (SJ 543413). The church (now URC) originated in 1798 as a secession from the Presbyterian congregation, the seceders first meeting in a small building on the present site. The chapel was rebuilt in 1845–6 and has brick walls with a rusticated ashlar front and slated roof. The front, of yellow sandstone, is pedimented and has an open porch of three bays with two Roman Doric columns carrying an entablature inscribed 'Congregational Chapel 1846' and three round-arched windows above; the side walls of four bays have round-arched upper windows. The window frames, formerly hung sashes, were replaced c.1900 and the interior of the porch altered. Galleried interior with original seating.

Elliot (1898) 88–94: Tomalin, R. W., *Dodington Congregational Church, Whitchurch, Shropshire, 1798–1948* (1948).

(115) Former WESLEYAN, St Mary's Street, Whitchurch (SJ 542416). Rendered walls and hipped slate roof, front of three bays divided by pilasters with a pediment over the middle bay, plain Venetian window above central doorway, round-arched windows at sides, lower front windows altered for post-office use. Built 1810 and superseded 1879 by a Gothic chapel in St John's Street.

WORTHEN

(116) BAPTIST, Lordshill (SJ 380020). Baptists who had formerly been united with Independents at Minsterley (see (56) above) built a chapel here 'close to Snailbeach Mines' in 1833. The present chapel, which has rendered walls and a tiled roof, was built in 1873; it has a gabled front with round-arched windows. A cottage adjoins to the right. *Baptistery*: a flight of steps NW of the chapel leading down to a stream appears to indicate the first baptizing place; a later external baptistery lies SW of the chapel. *Monuments*: in burial-ground in front of chapel (1) Thomas Young, 1857, and Martha his wife, 1836; (2) Martha, 1838, and Anne, 1847, daughters of Edward and Mary Eveans.

Elliot (1898) 138.

(117) PRIMITIVE METHODIST, Aston Rogers (SJ 342064). Three-bay front; opened 1845.

(118) PRIMITIVE METHODIST, Snailbeach (SJ 372021). Rubble and slate, lancet Gothic with gabled front, 1876.

STAFFORDSHIRE

The county is notable for two major conurbations, centred on Wolverhampton, Walsall and West Bromwich in the south and on Stoke-on-Trent in the north. In both of these districts, the result of rapid industrial expansion in the 19th century, many chapels were erected; but whereas in the latter numerous examples, particularly of Methodist architecture, are to be found, the former has retained little of consequence. The Congregational chapel at Mayers Green, West Bromwich, of 1807, demolished in the course of road improvements, is one of the more recent losses, while mention must also be made of the former Presbyterian Chapel in John Street, Wolverhampton, of 1701, which figures in the historically important 'Wolverhampton Chapel Case' of 1817, in which the Unitarian trustees and congregation were dispossessed after a protracted and expensive legal battle.

The oldest remaining Presbyterian meeting-houses in the county, at Dudley (31) (until recently a detached portion of Worcestershire), Newcastle (68) and Stafford (79), suffered severely in the Sacheverell riots of 1715, the first two having to be entirely rebuilt. All, including Tamworth (96), of slightly later date, were greatly altered in the 19th century or later. The four Friends' meeting-houses (27), (58), (81), (102) are small buildings of which the latest, at Stafford, of 1730, is the most complete. Also in Stafford, the Brethren's meeting-room of 1839–40 (80), is noteworthy as one of the few buildings remaining from the opening years of the movement. The various branches of Methodism are well represented throughout the county and the early spread of Primitive Methodism from the site of the first camp meeting at Mow Cop on the borders of Cheshire is evidenced by the presence at Cloud (78) of perhaps the oldest chapel of that denomination still in use. Amongst the more prominent early 19th-century Methodist chapels are those in the pottery towns of Burslem (85), Hanley (89) and Stoke (93), and at Merrial Street, Newcastle (70) the Wesleyan chapel of 1857–8, by James Simpson, is a worthy representative of the later period. A few Congregational chapels of 1840–50 are of interest, including King Street, Dudley (32) in a stuccoed Classical style, and Burton (19) and Cheadle (22) where Gothic was preferred; of wider importance are the two patronage chapels at Armitage (7), of 1820, and Oakamoor (73), of 1878, the latter being a particularly successful design for its purpose.

Throughout the lowland areas of the county brick is used almost exclusively as a walling material, the earliest being at Stafford of 1689; the brown brick with brown glazed headers at the New Meeting-house, Tamworth, (96), of 1724, is a local characteristic, but in the later 19th century the use of polychromatic brickwork is little in evidence. Tiles predominate as a roofing material although slate spread rapidly throughout the country. In the higher regions to the north-east around Leek, at the southern tip of the Pennines, good building stone is found in use in many small and sometimes remote chapels, and the Friends' meeting-house in Leek (58) was, when erected in 1697, a typical example of the Pennine vernacular style.

ABBOTS BROMLEY

(1) CONGREGATIONAL (SK 080244). Brick and slate, built 1824. Two pointed-arched windows in W gable wall with blocked doorway between, similar windows in N wall, low porch at E end. Original pulpit. *Monument*: in burial-ground, to Sarah wife of Eustace Sammons, 1846, small terracotta headstone.

ALDRIDGE-BROWNHILLS   *West Midlands*

(2) CONGREGATIONAL, Brownhills (SK 042059). Brown brick and slate with three-bay gabled front dated 1858, superseding chapel of 1830 which was then converted to a day school. Sunday-school to right; red brick with blue bands, 1868. (Proposed conversion to warehouse 1982)
     CYB (1860) 256.

ALREWAS

(3) Former WESLEYAN, (SK 168150), SE of Kents Bridge. Brick with a hipped tiled roof, built in 1805 and extended to the N in 1846. In the late 19th century it was converted to a school-house and the interior entirely refitted. Traces of pointed-arched windows, now blocked, remain in the E and W walls and at the N end, with smaller windows at each end of a former N gallery. The roof has king-post trusses.

(4) Former PRIMITIVE METHODIST, William IV Road (SK 172151). Brick with round-arched windows. Built 1828.

ALSTONEFIELD

(5) PRIMITIVE METHODIST, Milldale (SK 139548). Small chapel of rendered stone, tiled roof. Dated 1835.

ALTON

(6) PRIMITIVE METHODIST (SK 072423). Red brick on ashlar plinth, tiled roof; date-tablet 1826.

ARMITAGE WITH HANDSACRE

(7) ARMITAGE CHAPEL (SK 078162). Congregational services commenced in 1811 in a private house and the present chapel was built in 1820 apparently by Thomas Birch of Armitage Lodge

rendered dressings and a tiled roof. It comprises, besides the body of the chapel, a N aisle, E vestry and W porch; a schoolroom was added to the NE in the later 19th century. The W front has a gabled porch of two stories with angle-buttresses, a four-centred arched doorway with square label and shield-shaped stops and traceried wheel window above. The principal W gable behind is crowstepped and flanked by gabled diagonal buttresses. The S

ARMITAGE CHAPEL

who placed it in trust for Congregationalists in 1831 (now URC). It is of particular interest as an example of patronage building in which the orientation and the diversity of building elements appear to indicate the advanced aspirations of the original proprietor, who in 1831 retained the right of burial in a private vault under the N aisle. The chapel has brick walls with

wall, of two principal bays, is divided by two-stage buttresses and has large rectangular windows with moulded labels. The E vestry has a S doorway with two-centred arched head and moulded label, and two pointed-arched windows in the E wall. The N aisle has a two-centred arched W doorway in a gabled projection.

Armitage Chapel
ARMITAGE WITH HANDSACRE
Staffordshire

5 0 5 10 15 20 Feet

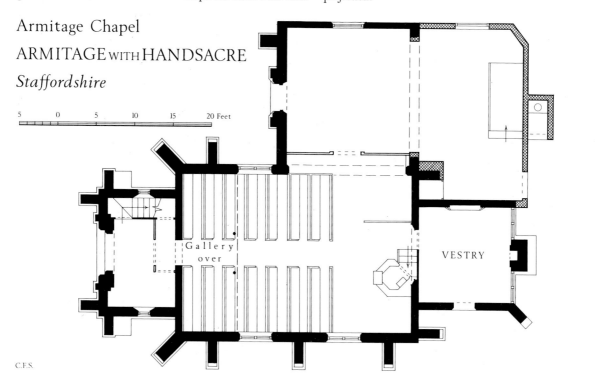

Gallery over

VESTRY

N

C.F.S.

The interior of the chapel has a segmental barrel-vaulted ceiling with two exposed tie-beams surmounted by arcading; a four-centred arch at the E end, resembling a small chancel arch, is closed by a pair of panelled wooden doors opening to the vestry with the pulpit in front of the S door. A four-centred arched opening to the N aisle has been closed by a later wooden screen. At the W end is a gallery with panelled front approached by a staircase in the W porch.

Fittings – *Clock*: on front of gallery, brass face, signed 'Parkinson, London', early 19th-century. *Monuments*: on W wall of N aisle (1) Thomas Birch of Armitage Lodge, 1837; (2) Mary, widow of Thomas Birch, 1842, pair of white marble tablets surmounted by urns; in burial-ground S of chapel (3) James Matthews, 1841, Mary his wife, 1830, *et al.*, table-tomb; (4) Louisa Ibotson, 1825. *Pulpit*: octagonal, with panelled sides, moulded base and cornice, *c*.1820. *Seating*: in gallery, original pews with panelled backs; lower seating renewed late 19th century.

ASHLEY

(8) CONGREGATIONAL (SJ 759367). Brown brick and tile with simple pediments to front and rear and date-tablet of 1841.

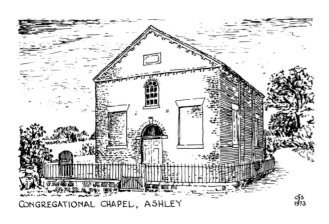

CONGREGATIONAL CHAPEL, ASHLEY

cfs 1973

Lower vestry wing behind built 1868. *Monuments*: in burial-ground (1) William Furnival, 1848, and James Unett Furnival, 1849 died at Forzapore, Bengal; (2) Alice Dunn, 1849; (3) Thomas Ward, 1849, William his son, 1845, *et al.*

(9) WESLEYAN, Wesley Road (SJ 753368). Originally three bays. Large tablet of 1860 over former entrance records gift of land by T. Astin.

(10) INDEPENDENT METHODIST, Hookgate (SJ 746351). Brick with four-centred arched windows; tablet 'Providence Chapel 1881' above entrance incorporates clock face.

(11) PRIMITIVE METHODIST, Hookgate (SJ 744353). Gabled front inscribed 'Primitive Methodist Jubilee Chapel 1860'.

AUDLEY RURAL

(12) WESLEYAN, Old Road, Audley (SJ 803511). Pedimented front with round-arched windows; dated 1876.

BAGNALL

(13) CONGREGATIONAL, Tompkin (SJ 944513). Built 1865, on site of chapel opened 1837. *Monument*: in burial-ground, to William Turner, 1839, and Ann his wife, 1838. (URC)

BARTON-UNDER-NEEDWOOD

(14) WESLEYAN (SK 187188). Rendered brick walls and slate roof hipped to front. Two round-arched windows with intersecting glazing bars and oval tablet ' . . . Ebenezer 1828', above later porch.

BLORE WITH SWINSCOE

(15) PRIMITIVE METHODIST, Swinscoe (SK 132481). Rubble and tile, lean-to porch against E gable wall covers original entrance, tablet over dated 1835.

BRADNOP

(16) WESLEYAN, School Lane (SK 012552). Squared stone with ashlar dressings. Large tablet above S entrance dated 1840. (Much altered since 1973)

BRANSTON

(17) CONGREGATIONAL (SK 222211). Rendered front with lancet windows; dated 1834. Small Sunday-school opposite *c*.1860. (URC)

BREWOOD

(18) WESLEYAN, Coven (SJ 909065). Low gabled front dated 1839.

BURTON UPON TRENT

(19) Former CONGREGATIONAL, High Street (SK 252232). The church which met here until *c*.1973 originated as a Presbyterian congregation gathered in the late 17th century by Thomas Bakewell, ejected Rector of Rolleston, Staffs. In 1803 the meeting-house was let to Independents and the trust deed was subsequently altered in their favour. The present chapel, opened 20 September 1842 to replace a building registered in 1708, is said to incorporate some re-used materials from the recently demolished racecourse grandstand.

The chapel has walls of brick with an ashlar front and a slated

roof. The E front has an arched centre bay flanked by buttresses perhaps once surmounted by pinnacles, opening to a porch with a four-light traceried window at the back and entrances in the return walls to N and south. *Monuments*: in front of chapel, slate headstones, (1) Rev. James Peggs, 1850, former missionary at Cuttack, Orissa, and four years General Baptist pastor in Burton; (2) Elizabeth Bakewell, 1838, 'lineal descendant of the Revd. Thos Bakewell, Rector of Rollestone... ejected 1661'.

    CHST III (1907–8) 81–7: *Evangelical Magazine* (Nov. 1842) 550: Matthews (1924) III, 168–9, 219 and *passim*.

CANNOCK

(20) WESLEYAN, Chapel Lane, Cannock Wood (SK 042123). Rendered walls, round-arched windows. Opened 1834.

CHAPEL AND HILL CHORLTON

(21) Former WESLEYAN, Hill Chorlton (SJ 801394). Rendered brick walls and slate roof. Oval tablet inscribed 'Wesleyan Chapel. The land kindly granted by his Grace the Duke of

Sutherland. 1834'. Converted to house 1971 and chapel windows altered.

CHEADLE

(22) CONGREGATIONAL, Tape Street (SK 010433). The original chapel standing behind the present building is a plain structure of brick with a tiled roof ($30\frac{1}{4}$ft by $26\frac{3}{4}$ft externally); it was erected in 1799 and the remains of a round-arched window of this date survive in the NW wall; it was enlarged by $6\frac{1}{2}$ft to the SW and refronted in 1821.

Present chapel.   *Photograph © Staffs. C.C.*

    The present chapel, which like its predecessor is named 'Bethel', was built in 1850 in a simple Gothic style to the designs of John Holmes, 'architect and builder' (see monument (3) below). The walls are of red brick with stone dressings and the roof is slated. A shield-shaped tablet in the main gable bears the date of erection. *Monuments*: in burial-ground (1) John Mellor, 1830; (2) William Bennett, 1835, *et al.*; (3) John Holmes, 1858, builder, Lucy his first wife, 1852, and Hannah his second wife, 1867, slate headstone.

    CYB (1851) 258–9.

(21) CHAPEL AND HILL CHORLTON. Former Wesleyan chapel. Before and after conversion to house.

CHEBSEY

(23) Former WESLEYAN, Norton Bridge (SJ 871301). Dated 1859. Original cast-iron railings in front. (Windows altered and railings removed since 1973)

CHECKLEY

(24) PRIMITIVE METHODIST, Fole (SK 044374). Brown brick with hipped tiled roof; three-bay front, dated 1850.

(25) PROVIDENCE CHAPEL, New Road, Upper Tean (SK 009396). Congregational services commenced in 1770 and the present chapel was built in 1822. Three-bay gabled front of red brick with central doorway and two tiers of windows. *Monument*: in front of chapel, to Mary, wife of James Burton, 1834.

(26) WESLEYAN, New Road, Upper Tean (SK 009397). Brick and slate; dated 1843.

CHEDDLETON

(27) Former FRIENDS (SJ 989512), SW of Basford Hall. The meeting-house was built in 1695–7 on a site acquired in 1693. It

is a small building (20¾ft by 15¼ft) with stone walls and a tiled roof. The entrance is centrally in the W wall and traces of original windows remain in the N and S gable walls.

The former *burial-ground* to the S, initially 20 yards by 10 yards, was granted to Friends in 1667 and continued in use until 1828. It is now an irregular enclosure with low stone boundary walls rising a few feet above the surrounding ground; there are no monuments.

Stuart (1971) 40–1.

(28) WESLEYAN (SJ 971523). Brick and tile, mostly concealed behind later building. Original doorway and windows in N wall. Date-tablet, loose, inscribed 'Wesleyan Chapel, 1849'.

COLWICH

(29) MOUNT ZION CHAPEL, Great Haywood (SJ 999225). Congregational, of red brick with stone dressings and a tiled roof, built 1845. Gabled front with round-arched doorway in plain gabled stone surround and two tiers of round-arched windows, the upper pair blind, with moulded labels. The design similar to (95) below. *Monuments*: S of chapel, to James Whittle, 1849.

DENSTONE

(30) PRIMITIVE METHODIST, Stubwood (SK 096400). Stone and slate; dated 1841.

DUDLEY   *West Midlands*

(31) THE OLD MEETING-HOUSE, Wolverhampton Street, Dudley (SO 943902). The first meeting-house of the Presbyterian (latterly Unitarian) society, built in 1702, was destroyed in the Sacheverell riots of July 1715, in an account of which reference is made to 'the two great pillars that beare up the roofe'. The meeting-house was rebuilt at public expense and re-opened in 1717. It was drastically altered in 1869 when a new entrance was made at the NE end and the interior refitted.

The walls are of rubble with ashlar facing to the NW and a hipped slated roof. The NW wall has a stone plinth, platband and moulded eaves cornice; two windows in the end bays replace original entrances. The SE wall is similarly fenestrated but with timber lintels to the windows. Two tall round-arched windows

at the SW end replace two tiers of windows of which the upper lintels remain. The NE wall was rendered and an entrance-porch and organ-chamber added in 1869.

The interior (38ft by 48ft) has a gallery around three sides and pulpit at the SW end. Some 18th-century fielded panels are re-used as a dado and behind the gallery fronts. *Plate*: includes a pair of two-handled cups of 1751.

Evans: (1897) 77–8: Evans (1899) 101–21: *UHST* VI (1935–8) 158–9.

(32) CONGREGATIONAL, King Street, Dudley (SO 944901). The church (now URC) was formed in 1792. The chapel, of brick and slate rendered at the front with stucco, is dated 1840.

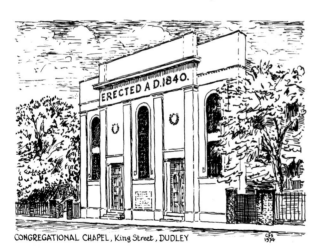

CONGREGATIONAL CHAPEL, King Street, DUDLEY

(33) BAPTIST, Ebenezer Street, Coseley (SO 940937). 'Ebenezer Chapel', brick and slate with rendered three-bay pedimented and pilastered front, is dated 1857. Side wall facing Birmingham New Road originally of four bays with two tiers of windows round-arched in blue and yellow brick.

(34) BAPTIST, Hospital Lane, Coseley (SO 937935). The former 'Providence Chapel', alongside Providence Row, of brick and slate, with simple pedimented front of three bays with two tiers

of round-arched windows, is dated 1809. Present chapel to W, 1870–1, by T. Richards.

(35) RUITON CHAPEL, Hermit Street, Lower Gornal (SO 919921), built in 1830 for a Congregational Church (now URC) formed in 1778, has walls of ashlar and a slated roof. The

SE front has terminal pilasters supporting a moulded cornice and pedimental gable. The previous chapel, built in 1778, had a broad front to the S with two doorways, a segmental-arched window between and gallery windows above.

SE of the chapel is a former school building of two stories with a fragmentary inscription reset close to the foot of an external stair with the date 1827.

Barnett, F. A. *et al.*, *Ruiton Congregational Church* (1972).

(36) METHODIST NEW CONNEXION, Ruiton Street, Lower Gornal (SO 918915). Rendered front with two tiers of round-arched windows; dated 1841.

(37) WESLEYAN, Mount Pleasant, Merry Hill (SO 924862). Rendered front much altered in late 19th century inscribed '1828/WESLEY'.

(38) METHODIST NEW CONNEXION, Northfield Road, Netherton (SO 950878). 'Providence Chapel', opened 1837, has brick walls covered with modern rendering. The gabled front, of three bays, has a central entrance with pilasters and two tiers of round-arched windows with cast-iron frames. A gallery around three sides is supported by slender fluted columns. (Re-erected 1978 in the Black Country Museum, Dudley. SO 948917)

(39) METHODIST NEW CONNEXION, St John Street, Netherton (SO 944881). Built 1848, enlarged to the rear in 19th century and refronted 1903.

(40) METHODIST NEW CONNEXION, High Street, Pensnett (SO 914892). Three-bay front with recessed centre inscribed 'ST. JAMES' CHAPEL 1837'. Sunday-school behind, built 1839, rebuilt 1928. (Demolition proposed 1982)

ECCLESHALL

(41) Former CHAPEL, The Horsefair (SJ 831290). Round-arched windows with intersecting glazing bars, and defaced tablet above altered entrance. Mid 19th-century.

FAWFIELDHEAD

(42) Former PRIMITIVE METHODIST, Hulme End (SK 103593). Limestone with sandstone dressings. Gabled front with rusticated quoins, round-arched doorway with fanlight, and partly defaced tablet of 1834. Side walls each with two windows with rusticated jambs.

(43) WESLEYAN, Newtown (SK 061633). Stone and tile, S front with tablet dated 1841. *Sundial*.

WESLEYAN CHAPEL, NEWTOWN, FAWFIELDHEAD
CFS 1973

(44) WESLEYAN, Rewlach (SK 094617). Stone and tile with contemporary porch dated 1849.

WESLEYAN CHAPEL, REWLACH, FAWFIELDHEAD
CFS 1973

FORSBROOK

(45) WESLEYAN, Boundary (SJ 982426). Brick and tile. Tablet on gabled side dated 1827.

HAMMERWICH

(46) PRIMITIVE METHODIST, Springhill (SK 072056). Gabled S front originally had central doorway between two round-arched windows. Entrance re-sited and inscribed tablet of 1844 altered.

HEATHYLEE

(47) PRIMITIVE METHODIST, Morridge Top (SK 032654). Small chapel at 1,500ft altitude, with stone walls and stone slate roof.

Opened 1850. Gabled entrance to S, two plain windows in each side wall.

(48) WESLEYAN, Upper Hulme (SK 013610). Gabled front with large tablet below upper window inscribed 'UPPERHULME/ SUNDAY SCHOOL/1838'.

HEATON

(49) WESLEYAN, Danebridge (SJ 965651). Stone and slate, on steeply sloping site with chapel at upper level. Two blocked windows in W wall suggest a major alteration or subdivision in the late 19th century. Tablet on E gable wall dated 1834.

HILDERSTONE

(50) WESLEYAN (SJ 949342). Built 1894; oval tablet inscribed 'J.WESLEY/Methodist Chapel/1822' reset in front wall.

HOLLINGSCLOUGH

(51) WESLEYAN (SK 065666). Walls of coursed rubble with ashlar dressings and a stone slate roof. The gabled front of three bays has two tiers of round-arched windows and a central doorway with rusticated surround; a tablet below the middle upper window is inscribed 'BETHEL/J ∗ L/1801', and in the gable is an oval recess pierced at the centre, perhaps intended to take the drive for a public clock. The interior has a rear gallery returning half-way along one side, with panelled front and early 19th-century seating. *Chandelier*: brass, six branches reduced to three, surmounted by a dove, early 19th-century. *Monument*: John Lomas, 1823, and Sarah his widow, 1833.

HORTON

(52) WESLEYAN, Gratton (SJ 934562). Three-bay chapel opened 1822, refronted with banded red brick in late 19th century.

IPSTONES

(53) 'CHAPEL HOUSE' (SK 005499) was built *c*.1790 as a private chapel by John Sneyd of Belmont Hall following a temporary dispute with the incumbent of St Leonards Church and subsequently converted to domestic use. It has walls of sandstone and a tiled roof, and comprises a nave and W tower. The nave has a large E window, now blocked, of four lights with cusped intersecting tracery in a two-centred arched head. Some traces of

former windows remain in the N wall. On the S side is a central doorway with chamfered jambs and two windows to the W with Y-tracery in two-centred arched heads; the lower of two windows to the E is also probably original. The W tower is of two stages with stepped buttresses and a pyramidal roof; the N and S walls have in each stage a pointed-arched window with Y-tracery.

(54) Former PRIMITIVE METHODIST (SK 023501). Stone walls with brick front and hipped tiled roof. The broad NW front of three bays has been altered but the tops of two pointed-arched windows with keystones remain flanking a tablet inscribed with the name and date 1837.

KINGSLEY

(55) PRIMITIVE METHODIST, Whiston (SK 036472). The former chapel of c.1840, standing opposite its successor of 1907–8, has stone walls with a brick front and tiled roof. The gabled front, now altered, originally had a parapet with ball finials and a round-arched doorway with tablet above.

LAPLEY

(56) CONGREGATIONAL, Wheaton Aston (SJ 852127). 'Zion Chapel', dated 1814, was enlarged to rear and much altered 1908.

LEEK

(57) CONGREGATIONAL, Derby Street (SJ 985565). Built 1862–3 in Decorated Gothic Style by William Sugden of Leek has a tower and spire above the principal entrance. It stands on the site of the formerly Presbyterian meeting-house occupied from the late 17th century which was rebuilt in 1780. (URC)
   CHST III (1907–8) 4–19; *CYB* (1864) 282–3: Matthews (1924) 132–3, 150–1.

(58) FRIENDS, Overton Bank (SJ 982566). Quaker meetings commenced in the mid 17th century; in 1693 land called 'Tranter's Croft' and some old buildings were bought and by 1697 the present meeting-house had been built. It was extensively altered in 1794 and enlarged to the E but traces of the former fenestration remain. The walls are of stone and the roof is tiled. The original building (approx. 30ft by 17ft) is aligned E–W. In the gabled W wall is a wide doorway and three-light mullioned window, both now blocked; in the N wall is a second narrower doorway with two windows to the W and two above, also blocked, and on the S side further windows at two levels probably replace original mullioned openings. The interior, now much altered, has at the W end the remains of a stand with a large hung-sash window behind it, and a gallery at the E end.
   Stuart (1971) 42: Sturge (1895) 19.

(59) WESLEYAN, Mount Pleasant (SJ 982567). Large chapel of brown brick with slate roof hipped to N, built 1811 and enlarged 1877 and 1891. The N front, of five bays, has a stone plinth, platband and cornice, and two tiers of round-arched windows; a central doorway has been inserted between the two original entrances and a pair of Tuscan columned porches in front of the latter have been united. The side walls have each four bays of windows with stone lintels. *Monuments*: in forecourt to N,

seven ledger stones including (1) Rev. Edward Jones, Wesleyan Minister, 1837; (2) Samuel Rowley, 1818; (3) William, son of William and Catherine Arnott, 1816, with indent of brass inscription plate.

LICHFIELD ST MARY

(60) CONGREGATIONAL, Wade Street, Lichfield (SK 118094). Opened 18 March 1812 by a congregation (now URC) formerly meeting in a room in Tunstall's Yard, Sandford Street. Brick

walls and a slated roof; front with a simple pediment and two tiers of windows. Gallery around three sides with panelled front. The pulpit and lower pews renewed, some original seating remains in gallery.
   Monuments: in chapel (1) Rev. David Griffiths, 1848; (2) Rev. William Salt, 1857; (3) William Daniel, 1829, 'one of the first members of the church assembling in this place'. (Demolition proposed 1978)
   Matthews (1924) 186–90.

LONGDON

(61) LONGDON GREEN CHAPEL (SK 087136), built by a Presbyterian, latterly Congregational, society and registered in 1696, was a plain brick building (30ft by 20½ft) with a tiled roof. It was demolished for road construction c.1965–70. Existing photographs show two late 17th-century windows in the N wall; a pair of taller windows on the S and a pointed-arched doorway in the W gable wall, apparently of c.1800, indicate later alterations for which George Birch of Armitage may have been responsible. *Monument*: William Edwards, 1775, 'Clerk of this Chappel', headstone.
   CHST III (1907–8) 33–47: Matthews (1924) 106, 125.

LONGNOR

(62) WESLEYAN, Buxton Road (SK 088650). Stone and slate, pedimented front with rusticated quoins and round-arched windows to lower stage; dated 1853 but perhaps incorporating part of an earlier structure.

(61) LONGDON. Longdon Green Chapel. *Photograph © Staffs C.C.*

MADELEY

(63) Former WESLEYAN (SJ 771442). Blue brick and tile, gabled front with oval tablet dated 1831.

(64) PRIMITIVE METHODIST (SJ 773449). 'Ebenezer Chapel' dated 1856.

MARCHINGTON

(65) PRIMITIVE METHODIST (SK 132308). Gabled front with small lancet windows. Dated 1841.

MILWICH

(66) WESLEYAN, Garshall Green (SJ 969341). Gabled front with narrow round-arched windows. Dated 1835.

MUCKLESTONE

(67) PRIMITIVE METHODIST, Knighton (SJ 730402). Low three-bay front with later porch and altered tablet dated 1834.

NEWCASTLE-UNDER-LYME

(68) THE OLD MEETING-HOUSE, Lower Street (SJ 846461). The Presbyterian, now Unitarian, congregation originated in the later 17th century when it was assisted by Rev. George Long, one of the ejected ministers. In 1694 a building 'on ground called the Fulatt' was registered as a meeting-house and this was superseded in 1717 by the present building, the former having been

The Old Meeting-house,

NEWCASTLE-UNDER-LYME, *Staffordshire*

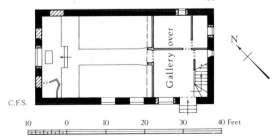

C.F.S.

10   0   10   20   30   40 Feet

destroyed by rioters on 14 July 1715. The congregation has had a very chequered existence, dying out and being re-formed on several occasions and the meeting-house was closed or put to other uses 1804–8, 1810–20, 1850–2, 1872–6 and c.1895–8. As a result the building has undergone numerous refittings and alterations, the latest in 1926 being the addition of an upper storey, and little of the original work remains visible.

The meeting-house, standing close NW of St Giles Church and claiming a right of access through the churchyard, has brick walls covered with a modern rendering and a tiled roof. The front wall facing SW has three segmental-arched windows and a doorway to the south-east. The interior ($42\frac{3}{4}$ ft by $20\frac{1}{2}$ ft) has a SE gallery with fielded panelled front of c.1717 and a staircase of similar date with moulded balusters and straight string; the pulpit and partitioning below the gallery incorporate re-used 18th-century panelling. A window centrally in the NW wall inserted c.1926 and containing late 19th-century glass from the Unitarian 'Church of the Saviour', Whitchurch, Shropshire, replaces two smaller windows.

Monuments: none now visible, but Pegler records, in floor below gallery (1) Hannah, wife of Tho. Astbury, 1729; (2) Lydia, wife of Humphry Borrow, 1731. *Sculpture*: on gallery front, portrait of Josiah Wedgewood, carved oak in enriched oval frame, by F. J. Saunders, 1910.

Pegler, G., *A History of the Old Meeting House, Newcastle-under-Lyme* [c.1924]: UHST V (1931–4) 393–410.

(69) CONGREGATIONAL, King Street (SJ 852462). Of 1859, by R. Moffat Smith. Built on a new site to replace 'the Marsh Chapel' occupied since c.1784 by a church formed in 1777 through the preaching of Captain Jonathan Scott. The walls are of yellow brick with bands of blue brick and stone dressings. In front is a large wheel-window above the entrance and a thin octagonal tower and spire at one corner.

CYB (1860) 245: Matthews (1924) 132, 234.

(70) Former WESLEYAN, Merrial Street (SJ 850462). 'Ebenezer Chapel' of 1857–8 by James Simpson has walls of red brick with

stone dressings and a slate roof. The front has a stone plinth, platband and pediment. Inside is a continuous rounded gallery. (Converted to commercial use since 1978)

A former Wesleyan chapel, later United Methodist, in Lower Street, perhaps late 18th-century, has been demolished.

(71) PRIMITIVE METHODIST, Higherland (SJ 846457). Brick and tile with pedimented centre bay inscribed 'Rebuilt A.D. 1853'; perhaps incorporating work of the early 19th century. Sunday-school behind dated 1836.

NEW CHAPEL

(72) WESLEYAN, Mow Cop (SJ 856570). Large chapel of ashlar with a hipped roof, broad S wall of three bays with two tiers of round-arched windows and tablet above entrance inscribed

'WESLEYAN/1852'; a second, larger, entrance at a higher level at the W end is flanked by two tall windows.

OAKAMOOR

(73) BOLTON MEMORIAL CHAPEL (SK 054451), opened 21 April 1878, was built by Alfred Sohier Bolton, proprietor of a local brass and copper wire works, for an Independent church

which originated in 1867. It is a highly finished 'patronage chapel' of stone in the Gothic style of Edward F.C. Clarke, comprising a continuous nave and chancel, N vestry, S organ-chamber and porch, W vestry and W porch, with a bell-cote above the W gable. Original fittings include a stone pulpit and font and a carved wood eagle lectern.

Glass: in E window with symbolic figures of Life, Immortality and Hope, given 1878. *Inscription*: in W vestry on painted board, recording the erection and opening of the chapel and inclusion of the 'Te Deum' in the order of service. *Monuments*: in chapel on W wall (1) A.S. Bolton 'founder of this Chapel', 1901; W of chapel (2) A.S. Bolton, 1901, *et al.*, tall Celtic cross of granite.

ONECOTE

(74) PRIMITIVE METHODIST (SK 049550). Gabled front with tablet dated 1822, porch added 1934; tablet of 1843 on S wall perhaps records a refacing.

QUARNFORD

(75) WESLEYAN, Flash (SK 024672). Stone with hipped slate roof, broad three-bay front with two tiers of chapel windows

above basement storey and central doorway approached by double flight of steps. Tablet above entrance dated '1784...rebuilt 1821'. Two blocked windows in side wall perhaps remain from earlier chapel.

ROCESTER

(76) Former GENERAL BAPTIST (SK 107393). Brown brick with

hipped slate roof and three-bay front; altered tablet above entrance, dated 1837. Now Roman Catholic.

Wood (1847) 230.

RUGELEY

(77) WESLEYAN, Brereton (SK 053165). Built 1872; oval stone tablet from former chapel of c.1809 reset in gable.

RUSHTON

(78) PRIMITIVE METHODIST, Cloud (SJ 910624). A low building of stone with a tiled roof, opened in 1815 and one of the earliest to be built by this denomination. It has three windows in

the E wall and an entrance in the S gable wall now covered by a recent extension. The N and S gables have shaped kneelers.

Kendall (1905) I, 170.

STAFFORD

(79) PRESBYTERIAN, Mount Street (SJ 920234). The congregation (now URC) originated in the late 17th century when they were supported by the Rev. Noah Bryan, an ejected minister. In the late 18th century a minister was appointed from the Church of Scotland and in 1836 the building was referred to as the 'Scotch Church'. The meeting-house built in 1689 still remains although damaged by rioters in 1715 or 16, enlarged to the N in 1835–6 and to the S in 1899–1901. The walls are of brick with stone dressings and the roofs are tiled, except the N wing which is slate covered.

The original meeting-house, aligned E–W, is greatly obscured by the later work but the W end is unaltered apart from the substitution of a large traceried window and has a moulded plinth, ashlar quoins, moulded eaves cornice and a hipped roof. A gable has been added to the E end. The original broad S front remained until 1899 and had a pair of windows flanking the pulpit and entrances at each end. The interior (20¾ft by 41¼ft) had E and W galleries, now removed. The 1835–6 extension designed by Messrs Boulton and Palmer produced a T-shaped plan with a N wing equal in length to the older part and at right angles to it, with tall round-arched windows and an entrance at the N end. In the enlargement begun in 1899 a square S wing was added with a tower and short spire above a SE entrance, the seating pattern was reversed, the N wing was subdivided leaving a short chancel with schoolroom beyond and the interior refitted. *Royal Arms*: in glazed frame, after 1837.

Black (1906) 294–5: Drysdale (1889) 561–6.

(80) THE ROOM, St Mary's Place (SJ 921231), 50 yards SW of St Mary's Church, is one of the earliest meeting-rooms to be built for the Brethren. The assembly originated in 1838 and soon attracted the support of the Presbyterian minister, Rev. Alexander Stewart, who transferred his allegiance to the new society. 'The Room', built 1839–40, has brick walls and a slate roof, with wide eaves and a pediment at the N end. A modern N porch supersedes two segmental-arched entrances in the end bays of the E wall facing Church lane; the three intermediate bays on

the E side project slightly and have two tiers of windows with stone lintels. Minor rooms to the S were added in 1906 and 1927 and the interior was entirely refitted in 1930.

Monuments: loose in yard N of N porch, headstones, include (1) Charles Rowley, 1840, and Charlotte Rowley, 1846; (2) William Bayley, 1848.

Rowdon, H. H., *The Origins of the Brethren* (1967) 176.

(81) FRIENDS, Foregate Street (SJ 920237). The meeting-house, built in 1730 to the designs of Edward Frith on land which had been in use as a Friends' burial-ground since the late 17th century, is a small building of brick with a tiled roof, gabled to N

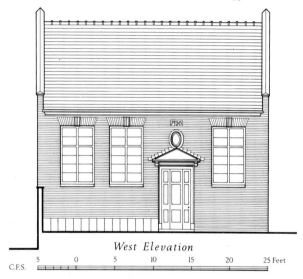

Friends' Meeting-house , STAFFORD
Staffordshire

West Elevation

C.F.S.   5   0   5   10   15   20   25 Feet

and south. The W front wall has windows with shaped keystones and a doorway with original frame and shaped brackets supporting a renewed pedimented canopy over which is an oval window and the date 1730 in raised characters. The E wall is mostly covered by a hall added in 1892 but one original window remains internally at the N end.

The interior (27¾ft by 18½ft) has a gallery at the S end with panelled front and staircase at the SW corner with turned balusters and a straight string. The stand at the opposite end is of one stage with two steps E and west. An attic room approached from the gallery by a winding stair in the SE corner is lit by a single window in the S wall and has a small fireplace adjacent. The roof has one truss with tie-beam and collar-beam.

Sturge (1895) 19–20.

(82) Former PRIMITIVE METHODIST, Gaol Road (SJ 921235). Three-bay pedimented front with giant pilasters, and pediments to former central entrance and lower windows. Built 1848; now Masonic Hall.

STANTON

(83) PRIMITIVE METHODIST (SK 125463). Above entrance '. . . Erected at the sole Expence of David Smith A.D. 1824'.

STOKE-ON-TRENT

(84) Former METHODIST NEW CONNEXION, Waterloo Road, Burslem (SJ 871495). 'Bethel Chapel' dated 1824 with rendered brick walls and slate roof has a front of five bays with pedimented centrepiece, round-arched upper windows, and wide porch. Two wings each of three storeys were added in 1835 and 'The Dr Coke Memorial School' at the rear, in polychrome brickwork, dates from the late 19th century.

(85) FREE METHODIST, Westport Road, Burslem (SJ 866498). The large 'Hill Top' Methodist chapel, also designated 'Burslem Sunday School' of brick with a slate roof, is of three storeys with the principal entrance approached by a double flight of steps and covered by a colonnaded porch of eight Greek Doric columns.

The front and sides are of five bays; a polygonal apse at the rear has a blocked Venetian window at the upper stage. Built 1836–7 to the designs of Samuel Parch. (Demolition proposed 1978–81)

(86) Former METHODIST NEW CONNEXION, Elder Road, Corbridge (SJ 876488). 'Providence Chapel', of 1884, now in industrial use, incorporates in the front wall an oval tablet of 1822 from the gable of its predecessor.

(87) WESLEYAN, Etruria Road, Etruria (SJ 868471). Three-bay rendered front with circular tablet dated 1820, stucco dressings later.

(88) HOPE CHAPEL, New Hall Street, Hanley (SJ 881478), built in 1812 for an Independent congregation which had recently seceded from The Tabernacle, was altered internally in 1891. The

walls are of brick and the roof is slated. The front wall has two doorways with fanlights and columned surrounds. (Reported demolished *c*.1975)

(89) METHODIST NEW CONNEXION, Albion Street, Hanley (SJ 882473). The large 'Bethesda Chapel' occupies the site of a preaching-house erected in 1798 soon after the formation of the Connexion. That building was enlarged in 1813 by about 10 yards with a circular end and gallery behind the pulpit. This is reported to have been replaced in 1819–20 by the present building for which the plans were drawn up by Mr Perkins, a schoolmaster. In 1856 the pulpit and communion-rail were renewed to designs by Robert Scrivener and in 1859–60 the chapel was refronted.

The walls are of red brick with yellow brick headers in Flemish bond and the roof is slate covered; the front wall is rendered in stucco. The rear part of the building, which is wider than the front, has a curved back wall with two tiers of windows in eight bays and five-bay sides with round-arched entrances in

the foremost bays. The narrower front section, perhaps added in 1859, is four bays in length and has a burial crypt below; the elaborately detailed facade is of five bays with bracketed cornice, two tiers of windows and open pediment above a central Venetian window. The front entrances, now partly rearranged, are covered by a loggia with colonnade of eight Corinthian columns reminiscent of that at Burslem Sunday-school (85). The interior, refitted in the late 19th century, has a continuous round-ended gallery and octagonal pulpit in an oval communion area.

Beyond the extensive burial-ground to the S is the School; of twelve bays with central pediment and octagonal lantern, and pedimented W end with inscriptions recording its erection in 1819 and enlargement in 1836. *Monument* in crypt, Rev. William Driver, 1831.

Smith, H. & Beard A., *Bethesda Chapel, Hanley* (1899).

(90) INDEPENDENT, Caroline Street, Longton (SJ 912437). Rebuilt 1905, circular tablet of 1819 from former chapel reset in side wall. (URC)

(91) METHODIST NEW CONNEXION, Lightwood, Longton (SJ 923415). Three-bay gabled front with circular tablet inscribed 'MOUNT ZION/1816'.

(92) Former INDEPENDENT, Aquinas Street (previously Thomas Street), Stoke-on-Trent (SJ 874453). Built in 1823 but sold to the Society of Friends in 1832 who continued to use it until 1951. It is of a single storey with brick walls, gabled to the N, with two windows in this wall and three at the E side with the entrance at the S end of the E wall. Burial-ground to E with flat marker-stones. (Derelict 1973)

Stuart (1971) 44–5: Sturge (1895) 20–1.

(93) WESLEYAN, Epworth Street, Stoke-on-Trent (SJ 875452). A large chapel of brick and slate, dated 1816, stands on a sloping site with windows to basement rooms at the E end. The W wall has a wide round-arched entrance flanked by pairs of windows. The longer N wall facing Hide Street is of five bays with two tiers of windows; the three slightly projecting middle bays are pedimented and have a former doorway at the centre from which a flight of steps has presumably been removed.

The interior has a continuous gallery with an organ recess at the E end, perhaps the site of a communion area behind the pulpit. The *pulpit* is an unusually elaborate structure of wood in

(93) STOKE-ON-TRENT. Wesleyan chapel, Epworth Street. Interior from W.

the Gothic manner supported by clustered pillars and ogee arches with vaulting beneath, and approached by twin staircases (see p. 224). The small *communion table* is in a similar style. *Fontlet*: pottery, copy of St Mary Magdalene, Oxford. *Monument*: David Bostock, 1820, 'ironfounder of this town', Mary his widow, 1830, *et al*.

(94) Former METHODIST NEW CONNEXION, Tower Square, Tunstall (SJ 859512). Rendered pedimented front of three bays, lower story converted to shops, built 1823–4.

STOWE

(95) Former CONGREGATIONAL, Hixon (SK 001257). The chapel, latterly Wesleyan, with altered date-tablet of 1842, closely resembles that at Great Haywood (29). It has red brick walls and a tiled roof. The gabled N front has a round-arched doorway in a gabled surround and two tiers of windows all with round-arched heads and moulded brick labels.

TAMWORTH

(96) THE NEW MEETING-HOUSE, Victoria Road (SK 209041). The Presbyterian, latterly Unitarian, society founded in the late 17th century erected their new meeting-house in 1724 on a site behind houses on the NE side of Colehill, which street long remained its principal or only approach. The building was re-roofed and drastically altered internally in 1879–80, and more recently a new entrance has been made in the SE side and the whole of that wall, exposed by the demolition of adjoining buildings, rendered and the window frames renewed.

The walls are of brown brick with darker glazed headers in Flemish bond and the roof is hipped and slate covered. The original entrance at one corner of the SW wall has been blocked, as has a corresponding doorway at the opposite side which led to the burial-ground and a new entrance and porch substituted *c*.1880 above which is a tablet inscribed 'THIS HOUSE/WAS BUILT/1724'. The NW wall is largely unaltered and has two tiers of segmental-arched windows with wooden cross-frames, three of which have opening lights with fretted escutcheons to the latches.

The interior (24ft by 42¼ft) may have had the pulpit against the SE side and galleries around, but no certain evidence remains. In 1879–80 the pulpit was re-sited at the NE end with a wooden screen of three pointed arches demarcating the line of the final bay.

Fittings – Monuments: on NW wall (1) John Lakin, 1860, and Elizabeth his widow, 1865; (2) Henry Lakin, 1846, and Anne Isabella his widow, 1863; (3) John Lakin, 1825, and Elizabeth his wife, 1824; (4) Sarah Lakin, 1831; (5) Rev. William Parkinson, 1857, 20 years minister; (6) Benjamin Shelton, 1833, and Catherine his wife, 1829; on SW wall (7) marble surround with urn, inscription panel lost; (8) Rev. John Byng, 1827, 53 years

Exterior from W.

Interior from S.
(96) TAMWORTH. The New Meeting-house, Victoria Road.

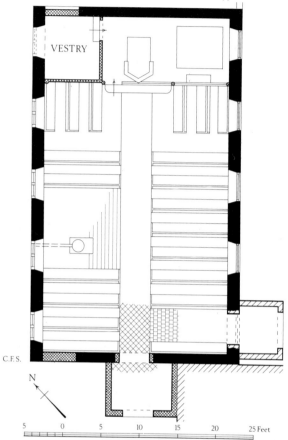

The New Meeting-house, TAMWORTH
Staffordshire

VESTRY

C.F.S.

N

5 0 5 10 15 20 25 Feet

pastor; (9) Henrietta, daughter of Rev. John Byng, 1827; on SE wall (10) Charles Harding, 1868, *et al.*; (11) Thomas Brittan Willcox, 1840; (12) William Harding, 1802, and Thomas son of William and Martha Harding, 1801; (13) Thomas Byng, 1822, Anne daughter of Thomas and Martha Byng, 1827, Thomas Gwyllym Byng, 1829, and Elizabeth Byng, 1829; (14) Joseph Clarson, 1831, Sarah his widow, 1860, and David their son, 1827. Nine of the above are signed by Mitchell of Tamworth.

Panelling: below side arches of NE arcade, four fielded panels with bolection-moulded edges, *c*.1724. *Pulpit*: four panelled sides with moulded cornice and base, from original pulpit; the railings in front incorporate 18th-century moulded balusters.

Evans (1897) 237: Evans (1899) 203–12.

(97) CONGREGATIONAL, Aldergate (SK 206042). Brick and slate dated 1827 but entirely refenestrated. Traces of two pedimented doorways remain on front wall now replaced by windows.

Sibree & Caston (1855) 336–44.

TITTESWORTH

(98) PRIMITIVE METHODIST, Thorncliff (SK 015584). Dated 1839.

TUTBURY

(99) CONGREGATIONAL, Monk Street (SK 212290). 'Ebenezer Chapel', built 1804–5, with brick walls rendered to the S and a slate roof, replaces a barn fitted up in 1799. It stands behind a forebuilding of brick with stone dressings and a central projecting turret (altered) added in the late 19th century when the chapel was refitted. Sunday-school to S dated 1884. *Monuments*: in burial-ground slate headstones, signed Brunt of Burton; Longhurst of Alrewas; and Shaw of Longford, include (1) Rev. Joshua Shaw, 1842, 32 years pastor at Ilkeston and Moorgreen, Derbys, and 12 years here, and Mary his widow, 1843; (2) Job Banister, 1839.

Matthews (1924) 183–5, 241.

(100) Former WESLEYAN, High Street (SK 213289). Three-bay gabled front with shaped tablet dated 1838.

UTTOXETER

(101) CONGREGATIONAL, Carter Street (SK 091334). Built 1827–8 superseding a meeting-house of 1792 in Bridge Street.

Brick and slate; front entrance with two Doric colums *in antis* to a formerly open lobby. Interior refitted 1887. (URC)

Elkes, L. M., *History of Congregational Church and Sunday School, Uttoxeter, 1788–1960* (1960).

(102) FRIENDS, Carter Street (SK 090333). The meeting-house built in 1705 on land given to the Society in 1700 was replaced by the present small building in 1770. The walls are of brick and the roof is tiled. The entrance was originally in the centre of the S wall facing the burial-ground flanked by two segmental-arched windows; in the 19th century the doorway was re-sited in the E gable wall and the former converted to a window. The E wall was partly rebuilt in 1961–2 when other major repairs were carried out. The interior ($25\frac{1}{4}$ft by 18ft) has a gallery at the E end

S front.

(103) UTTOXETER. Wesleyan chapel.

and a staircase with turned balusters and shaped finial to the bottom newel. The stand at the W end, removed 1961–2 and replaced by a single raised seat, formerly had a central entrance flanked by benches with shaped ends and tall backs of plank-and-muntin partitioning with newels as on the staircase. *Monuments*: in burial-ground (1) Samuel Botham, 1828 (father of the authoress Mary Howitt); (2) Harrison Alderson of Burlington, New Jersey, 1871.

Friends' Meeting-house, UTTOXETER
Staffordshire

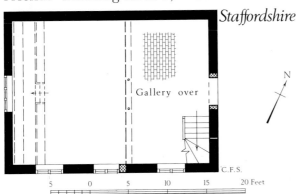

Gallery over

N

5   0   5   10   15   20 Feet

C.F.S.

(103) WESLEYAN, High Street (SK 091335). Brick, with three-bay gabled front; centre bay recessed with semicircular arch over, enclosing pedimented entrance, upper window and tablet dated 1812. Side walls of two bays extended one bay to rear. Interior with continuous gallery on iron columns partly refitted but with early 19th-century pulpit.

WALSALL   *West Midlands*
(104) WESLEYAN, Union Street, Willenhall (SO 964985). Built *c.*1836, front of five bays with domed corner towers added 1863–4; greatly altered. *Monument*: E of chapel, to James Carpenter, 1844, *et al.*

WEST BROMWICH   *West Midlands*
(105) PRIMITIVE METHODIST, Bell Street, Tipton (SO 951922). Opened 1823, much altered and extended to rear.

WOLVERHAMPTON   *West Midlands*
(106) Former STRICT BAPTIST, Temple Street (SO 913983). On S side of street. Brick and slate; opened 1796 by a church which, after suffering mixed fortunes and being re-formed on several occasions, was finally dissolved in 1955. The front wall has been entirely rebuilt but the rest remains little altered. The W wall has three arched recesses at an upper level. Two windows have been added at the S end. Now in industrial use.

Chambers (1963) 15–17.

(107) WESLEYAN, Darlington Street (SO 912986). Large chapel of brick and slate with rusticated stone dressings, built 1900–1 to designs by Arthur Marshall to replace a chapel of 1825. Pedimented N front between staircase bays surmounted by domed turrets. Galleried nave and transepts with apsidal choir gallery at S end and large lantern dome with mosaic-decorated pendentives above the crossing.

(108) PRIMITIVE METHODIST, Bath Street, Cinder Hill (SO 926943). Dated 1850. Brick and slate with round-arched windows; extended to rear.

WOOTTON
(109) Former PRIMITIVE METHODIST (SK 106451). The former chapel behind Tollgate Cottage has an ashlar front of three bays; the main windows, which had pointed-arched heads, have been altered and the doorway and a small window to the left blocked. Perhaps the conversion of an 18th-century cottage.

(93) STOKE-ON-TRENT. Wesleyan chapel, Epworth Street. Pulpit.